The Rosary

A Gospel Prayer

by
J. Patrick
Gaffney, S.M.M.

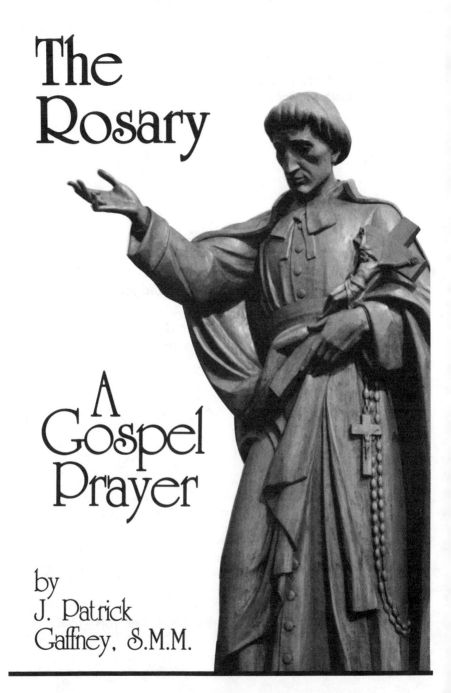

The Rosary

A Gospel Prayer

by
J. Patrick
Gaffney, S.M.M.

Reflections on the Rosary Mysteries
in the Spirit of Saint Louis de Montfort

Imprimatur
Most Reverend John R. McGann, D.D.
Bishop of Rockville Centre, N.Y.

To my brothers and sisters
whose love so beautifully
mirrors God
Margaret, Ed, Katherine and Joe,
Larry and Win,
Sister James and Sister Rosemary
from the Benjamin

Second printing 1999
Printed in the United States of America
ISBN 0-910984-56-5

Design: C. Micciche

© **Montfort Publications** Bay Shore, New York 11706

TABLE OF CONTENTS

INTRODUCTION

"I don't like to have the rosary shoved down my throat!" That was the angry complaint of a newly-appointed pastor who claims he was "cornered" by a group of "marian fanatics" trying to "force" him to have the rosary publicly recited before every Mass.

Two extremes concerning the rosary are found within the contemporary church. They appear to represent radically different views concerning marian devotion itself. One, growing steadily, proclaims dire, cataclysmic consequences if the rosary is not prayed daily. The well-being of the church, if not the very existence of planet earth is, they seem to say, in direct proportion to the number of rosaries recited. The other extreme either yawns at any mention of the rosary or angrily mumbles something like: "Why don't they push the eucharist instead!"

The first group generally founds their zeal in propagating the rosary solely on marian apparitions; whether approved or not makes little difference. The other flows from a gross misunderstanding of Mary's role in salvation history and of marian devotion itself.

Both extremes mentioned above are harmful. Both turn the faithful away from the rosary. They distort the true nature of the rosary and reflect an ignorance of the authentic scriptural portraits of the Mother of God.

How, then, should we view the rosary? The first statement to be made is: *The rosary can stand by itself without any props of private revelations.* Pope Paul VI, in his

7

decisive Apostolic Constitution, *On Devotion to the Blessed Virgin Mary*, beautifully and powerfully describes the nature of the rosary yet never once mentions any apparitions to support his claims. Never once in this most beautiful summary of the meaning of the rosary (42-55) is any mention made of calamities which will ensue if the rosary is not recited. Rather, the Holy Father concludes his rather lengthy study of the rosary with these words: "They (the faithful) should be drawn to its calm recitation by its intrinsic appeal." The rosary is so beautiful and is so highly recommended not because of any private revelations, not through fear of catastrophes, but precisely because, as the Popes have repeatedly declared, *it is a gospel prayer.*

As a gospel prayer, the rosary is the contemplation of God's infinite Love for us as disclosed in the great events of salvation history. The *Lord's Prayer, Hail Mary* and *Glory be...* form the background music, or the body of the rosary, creating a peaceful, prayerful atmosphere; the *soul* of the rosary is the contemplative immersion of the self into the great mysteries of God's victorious love. The rosary needs no apparitions or private revelations to authenticate it; although not to be ignored, they remain clearly secondary. In encouraging the prayerful recitation of the rosary we are not to begin with, *Our Lady at such-and-such an apparition demands it!* Rather, following the example of the magisterium, we must explain the rosary as the church understands it and invite others *to experience its prayerful recitation.*

The second statement is even more important: *The rosary — like all marian devotion — is Christ-centered.* Since the rosary is essentially scriptural, it necessarily intensifies our union with the climactic point of God's self-disclosure, Jesus the Lord. The rosary is a powerful means of arriving more intensely and more immediately at our goal, Jesus, through whom in the Spirit we are one with the Father.

Moreover, the rosary, as a loving contemplation of God's plan, leads to a more profound union with the Body of Christ, the church. A more authentic christian way of life is a consequence of the contemplative praying of the rosary. Its contemplative recitation strengthens our eucharistic, sacramental faith, for it "draws its motivating force from the liturgy and leads naturally back to it" as Paul VI teaches.

Both extremes mentioned above are among the "false devotions" which Saint Louis de Montfort so roundly condemns in 92-104 of his *True Devotion*. Let the rosary be understood and prayed according to the mind of the church and the faithful will, as Paul VI declares, be drawn to it by its "intrinsic appeal."

There are few "devotions" recommended by Saint Louis de Montfort. However, his life and writings make it clearly evident that the daily recitation of the rosary is a *distinctive and integral* mark of his spirituality. His fundamental reason for insisting on the rosary is a simple, balanced one, in line with the teaching of Paul VI: the rosary, as a contemplation of the mysteries of God's Love, is an extraordinarily effective means of entering more fully into Christ Jesus and becoming his instrument in evangelization.

There is a final comment which should be made before beginning the study of the rosary mysteries. *There is no one way of praying the rosary.* It adapts itself easily to the manner we pray, or to put it another way, to where we are in prayer. For some, each decade is a contemplative experience of a facet of the love of God; for others, each decade, or perhaps even each bead is prayed with a distinct mental image connected with the mystery. For many, it is a variation of one method and another. At times, some may be captured by the beauty of the background music itself, the prayers of the rosary. It is, therefore, as much a prayer for the contemplative monk as it is for the little child. Like all prayer, it demands perseverance and often struggle. Like all prayer, it can seem boring, useless. Like all prayer, it should become a personal, peaceful experience without tension or strain. The rosary should be a calming, re-creative break in the day's schedule.

It is hoped that the following reflections on the mysteries of the rosary, which first appeared in quite a different form in the marian review published by the Montfort Missionaries, *Queen of All Hearts*, may be of some assistance in praying the daily rosary "with attention and devotion, as if it were to be the last of my life" (Saint Louis de Montfort, *Methods for Saying the rosary*, in *God Alone, The Collected Works of Saint Louis Marie de Montfort*, p.238). The chapters are in the spirit of the teachings of Saint Louis de Montfort. They will especially reflect his christocentric mariology, his love for the mystery of the cross, his insistence on total consecration to the Eternal and Incarnate Wisdom, his strongly scriptural foundations. The vagabond missionary had all his belongings in a knapsack thrown over his shoulder; the Bible was always his most treasured possession and his writings and sermons are permeated with explicit or implicit quotes from the word of God.

The reflections examine *faith* as the general theme of the joyful mysteries, the *cross* as the characteristic of the sorrowful mysteries, the *glorious victory* of God's redemptive plan as the teaching of the glorious mysteries.

In the *Appendix* of this booklet will be found, excerpted from *On Devotion To the Blessed Virgin Mary*, the beautiful, normative teaching of Pope Paul VI on the rosary. Also included is the more popular method of praying the rosary advocated by Saint Louis de Montfort. For those not acquainted with the rosary, it may be well to read the *Appendix* before studying the theological meditations on the mysteries.

My deep thanks to my confrere, Father Roger Charest, s.m.m., the founder and Managing Editor of *Queen of All Hearts,* who suggested the compilation of this booklet. His love for our Lady and for our Father, Louis de Montfort, is without compare.

Father J. Patrick Gaffney, s.m.m., S.T.D.
Professor Emeritus Theological Studies
Saint Louis University
Editor, *Queen of All Hearts Magazine*
and Editor-in-Chief of JESUS LIVING IN MARY

The Joyful Mysteries
INTRODUCTION

Mary enjoys many titles. The Litany of Loreto invites us to respond with the calming, mantra-like "pray for us" to a sparkling array of names for this woman: Mother of God, Tower of David, House of Gold, City of David, Queen of All Saints - and the list goes on. All titles given to Our Lady have this in common: they glorify the Lord who has so freely gifted her and they inspire us to become more like her, totally centered on Jesus the Lord.

There is one marian title, however, which is becoming more popular in these days when the foundations of our christian faith are being challenged by the maxims of the "world". In the spirit of Pope John Paul's encyclical, *Mother of the Redeemer*, we turn to Mary, as the *Woman of Faith*. In a certain sense, this title is the most magnificent of all, for it is through her faith that Mary conceives the eternal Wisdom of the Father, it is through faith that she is the model disciple of the Lord, it is because of this active and responsible *Yes* to God's will that she is the spiritual mother of all the redeemed. *Mary, the Woman of Faith:* a beautiful summary of the grandeur of this woman.

When we examine the gospel portraits of Mary, it is her faith which appears to be the one color the Holy Spirit uses in depicting this woman. She is among those "who hear the word of God and keep it" (Lk 11:27-28); her words to the servants at the Cana marriage feast spring from her own faith: "Do whatsoever he tells you" (Jn 2:5). At the foot of the cross when all the apostles have deserted their Master, she and a small company keep faithful vigil. The crowds jeer and spit upon her, curse her as the mother of the criminal hanging on the cross. She remains faithful even to the end (Jn 19:25-27).

However, it is Luke's infancy narrative (Lk 1 & 2) - the overture to his proclamation of the public ministry of Jesus — which is nothing less than a treatise on faith through its description of Mary. Five principal episodes of these first two chapters of Luke's gospel directly involve Mary: the Annunciation, the Visitation, the Nativity, the Presentation in the Temple and the final section of the infancy narrative, the Finding in the Temple. These events — which have become the five joyful mysteries of the rosary — tell us the meaning of faith as it is lived by the first christian, the first disciple of the Lord. Far more appealing than an arid, speculative treatise on faith, these Lucan episodes illumine the meaning of christian faith through the living words and actions of our Lady. Meditation on these joyful mysteries discloses a woman ever more intensely centered on the Lord, a woman who is the exemplar of discipleship, the *Woman of Faith.*

It should be kept in mind that the Lucan infancy narrative, the source of the joyful mysteries, is clearly not a forgery. It is a divinely inspired authentic portrait. A portrait, in contrast to a snapshot, highlights the personality of an individual through embellishments of color, scenery, posture, etc. Often — as with the inspired literary portrait of Mary of the Lucan gospel — it is impossible to know precisely what embellishments an artist may have employed to clarify the personality of an individual. Nonetheless, when we contemplatively gaze at these scenes of the joyful mysteries, we are privileged to stand in awe before an authentic portrait of the incarnate Wisdom of the Father and of his Mother, Mary.

Faith knows no limits. It is not only trust in the Lord, it is not only believing in the truths revealed by God. Rather, it encompasses one's entire being. It is the fundamental, foundational gift of God to us. His creative Love, always present, empowers us to respond on every level of personality to his embedded call to center all on him. Faith is then, the lived-out response, on every level of personality to the Father, through Jesus the Lord, in the power of the Spirit. A person of faith sees everything, judges everything, measures everything, plans everything in the light of God's incarnate Wisdom, Jesus. Faith tolerates no idols. Wealth, prestige, power, sex, health, career, can all take center stage and so surreptitiously become idols. Yet, to find ultimate meaning outside of the Lord is to attribute to finite things or events an ultimacy which belongs only to God. *God Alone* was the battle cry of Saint Louis de Montfort as it must be of every christian. As Saint Augustine so beautifully wrote centuries ago: "Our hearts were made for you, O Lord, and they cannot rest until they rest in you."

In a certain sense, God has played a trick on us. God's love creates in us a yearning for eternal life, for never-ending love, for a fulfillment without end. And only God can bestow such magnificent gifts, for only God *is* Life, only God *is* Love. *The more we strive to fill our hearts with the goods of this world, the emptier we become.* Only the Infinite can fill the bottomless yearnings of the human heart.

Faith is, then, the living-out of the fundamental relationship of life, the relationship which must qualify all others: God is *for us,* and we are freely to surrender all to his Love. Faith unites heaven with earth, God with us, the Infinite with the finite, the Creator with the creature. Faith is to share in his Life of omnipotent Love, as God in Christ Jesus shares in our utter weakness.

The joyful mysteries of the rosary are nothing less than a profound contemplative study of faith, the foundation of our sharing in the divine nature (cf 2 Pet 1:4).

1
THE ANNUNCIATION

Any discussion on the central issue of *faith* can so easily become only speculation or nothing more than a "headtrip." What does faith mean in "real" life? If it is the totality of loving surrender, what are its practical consequences? Turn to the Annunciation narrative, Luke 1:26-38. The most profound and often cryptic theological explanations of faith come alive in Luke's divinely inspired description of Mary of the Annunciation, the first joyful mystery.

The scene is, of course, primarily Christological, i.e., it has as its principal purpose to tell us something about Jesus the Christ. He is the "Son of the Most High," "he will reign over the house of Jacob forever and of his kingdom there will be no end." The child shall be called "holy, the Son of God." With a few strokes of the pen, Luke has brought us to the heart of the mystery of salvation. God so loves this world that he is sending his own "Son," i.e., his own Life, his Word, his Wisdom, into this world. The evangelist tells us that this child will establish a "kingdom" which shall never end: the reign of Yahweh. The Son of God is entering our world so that he may appropriate our ruin and transform it into the kingdom. God is not only visiting the human family. Rather, in Jesus, God becomes one with his rebellious people, for the person of Jesus IS the Word of God. He who is Light now enters into our darkness and "the light shines in the darkness and the darkness has not overcome it" (Jn 1:5). The primary message of Luke is that Jesus is truly the enfleshed Son of God, *for us.*

There is another side to this portrait. Yes, its principal focus is on Jesus. However, there is also a magnificent portrayal of his mother, the one who accepts the Son of God into this world so that He may be our Redeemer and Savior. The first striking element of the portrait is the incredible condescension of our God. The Almighty does not force, does not destroy Mary's freedom. For God is Love (1 Jn 4:8). Love lures, love attracts, love calls. Love cannot force. God requests, therefore, through his messenger of salvation, Gabriel, the consent of Mary so that he may become our redeeming Brother. God enters into dialogue with Mary about this most important event in the history of creation. It is Mary whom God chooses to be the representative of this universe yearning for salvation; it is Mary who is to give her faith-consent, the *Yes* of the entire human race, to the inbreaking of Wisdom into our folly. Infinite Love knocks at the doors of this creation in such need of healing. It is our sister Mary who in the name of the entire human family, so broken, so lost, will swing open the gates so that the King of Glory may enter into our weakness transforming it into Life.

So often we think that Mary joyfully rushed to accept the privilege of becoming the mother of the Son of God. The Lucan portrait tells us otherwise. She is perplexed, confused by the greeting of the angel. She questions. In spite of the clarity with which the portrait depicts Jesus, Luke tells us in the final panel of his infancy portrait, that she did not understand (2:50). She knows enough at the Annunciation to give her active and responsible consent. She surely does not know all the details.

Faith is not, therefore, a response to a detailed plan presented to us by God. Far from it. Rather, it is a relationship to a Person, a relationship accepting that we are accepted by the Lord, a relationship which entails total obedience to the mysterious designs of Love itself. As with Mary, the Lord lets us know enough to make an active and

responsible consent to his call for total surrender to his love.
But the details? They remain hidden in his love. When a
couple is married, the husband and wife know enough to
make an active and responsible consent in order to share
their lives as symbols of God's love for us. But the details?
God in his mercy kindly conceals them. When young people enter religious life, at the time of the first profession little do they know of the details their commitment will bring.
Nonetheless, in surrendering to God's call, they are accepting all that flows from it, the joys and the sorrows, the difficulties and the pleasures. Mary of the Annunciation
teaches us a primary facet of faith: it is a total abandonment
to the inscrutable will of God, encompassing all that flows
from that loving surrender.

Not only does God not present us with all the details, but,
judging from his invitation to Mary, he tears up our plans as
he calls us to a total surrender. In light of the prevailing
custom, Luke appears to be telling us that Mary and Joseph
are already legally married at the time of the Annunciation:
"betrothed to a man whose name was Joseph." Betrothal in
the culture of Jesus' time cannot be equated with the
modern notion of "engagement." The "betrothal" is the
formal "I do" pronounced in the presence of witnesses.
After a waiting period of about six months to a year, the
groom would carry his bride over the threshold and they
would begin life together. However, even before this takes
place, the groom had legal rights over his wife and any
violation of those rights by the woman was apparently considered adultery.

It is during this interval between the "betrothal" and the
dwelling together that Mary, legally the wife of Joseph, is
visited by the Angel Gabriel. Her plans are clear. She is
awaiting that celebration when amidst the partying of the
village, Joseph will bring her to his house and they will live

happily ever after.

The theological teaching which is so prominent in the Annunciation portrait is that Mary must relinquish her plans in her total surrender to the Lord. *Yahweh is a God who tears up our plans.* Mary, the model of faith, must see her whole life totally at the disposal of the Lord. His designs are always greater than ours; nonetheless, it is so difficult to see our plans torn into shreds! But such is the way he calls Mary; such is the pattern of God. Without indicating to her the details of his plan, he requests Mary to leave all hers aside and to surrender to mysterious infinite Love.

The Annunciation of the Lord — which Montfort calls "a summary of all his mysteries" (*True Devotion,* 248) — discloses striking qualities about this call of God to faith. Since *everything we say about Mary we are ultimately saying about ourselves* as disciples of the Lord, the first joyful mystery tells us that God enters into dialogue with us. Through the sacrament of the present moment, through others, through the Scriptures, the eucharist, God calls, God lures, God attracts, God lets us know of his yearning to share life with us. Every second of the day bears the empowering call: "Follow Me!" In the portrait of Mary, we see ourselves. For we too are loved, we too are called to accept the overshadowing Spirit so that Christ may be formed within us.

It is also clear that faith in no way destroys our free will; rather it empowers us to praise God by actively and responsibly surrendering to him. In no way does God reveal the details of his providence for us; rather, requesting us to leave aside our own well thought-out plans, God asks for an acceptance of his loving designs even though the details are left unveiled. Truly, our God is a jealous God!

Mary's faith-response to this call from God to leave all aside and follow him is illustrative of the essence of faith itself. The Angel awaits Mary's answer. Love lures, calls, attracts, empowers. Mary's response is one of total surrender to Love, a consecration which entails discarding her plans and accepting a life which she herself never expected. There is anguish hidden in the portrait of this young girl as she responds to God. What of Joseph? What of the future? What of the Child? What of her reputation? How contrary to the gospel portraits of Mary to say that none of these questions tugged at her heart. Her sinlessness does not spare her from the pain involved in the destruction of her own plans — involving others whom she deeply loves — for the undetailed designs of God.

Her response? A clear *Yes* to God. She is the woman who hears the word of God and keeps it no matter the cost, no matter the heartache, no matter the consequences. So strongly does Luke want to depict this total consecration of Mary to the Lord that he places on this young girl's lips the expression which clashes head-on with modern values: "Behold the slave-girl of the Lord." Most English translations flinch from using such a term and substitute a watered down version, such as "handmaiden," "servant," as is done also for Mary's depiction of herself in the Magnificat (cf. Lk 1:48) where again Mary employs the term "slave." For Luke, the expression "slave" implies no servility, no cynical or wimpish acquiescence to an extravagant request. Rather, it denotes the totality of Mary's loving surrender to the Lord (cf *True Devotion*, 68-77). She is loved uniquely and she completely surrenders to that Love. Her whole personality, on every level of being is an active and responsible *Yes* to the Lord. She asks for nothing for herself, she makes no qualifications, requests no salary, no special privileges. A complete *Yes* is her simple reply. She belongs totally to the Lord. She is a woman of faith, the model christian, the paradigm of discipleship.

There is a final note in Mary's response. The expression "let it be done" implies that God's will is her wish. She freely opts to merge her will with that of the mysterious Love who is God. It is not a reluctant *Yes* or one which has a note of hurt or bitterness in it. Her final words summarize her being: "Lord, I am your loving slave-girl, belonging entirely to you without reserve; I yearn to do your will."

The core of faith is described in the Annunciation of the Lord to Mary, the first joyful mystery. As we gaze upon the beauty of the portrait, we should let the scriptures interrogate us, and then permit ourselves to be molded, interpreted by this effective and creative word of God. The model of faith, Mary, is not to be put into a niche on a side wall where no one can see her. Rather, we must join in her total consecration so that through the overshadowing Spirit we too may have the eternal Wisdom of God dwell within us.

May the grace of the mystery of the Annunciation come down into our hearts.

2
THE VISITATION

The inspired word insists that authentic faith must express itself in action. James scoffs at so-called christians who are "hearers only" and not "doers of the word." The blessings of God come only to the "doer that acts," for "he shall be blessed in his doing" (James 1:22-25). James vividly describes the ridiculous state of someone who claims total surrender to the Lord but does not live it: "What does it profit, my brethren, if a man says he has faith but has not works? Can his faith save him? If a brother or sister is ill-clad and in lack of daily food and one of you says to them, 'Go in peace, be warmed and filled,' without giving them the things needed for the body, what does it profit? So faith by itself, if it has not works, is dead...For as the body apart from the spirit is dead, so faith apart from works is dead " (James 2:14-17;26). As the body is the expression of the spirit, so too good works are the manifestation of faith. For if we believe in the Lord, then, as Matthew tells us, we will see him in the poor, the naked, the homeless, and hurry to his aid (cf. Mt 25:31-46).

When Paul, therefore, tells us that God "justifies him who has faith in Jesus " (Rom 3:26) and that "man is justified apart from works of law" (3:38), he is not contradicting the evangelical teaching that faith must express itself in action. Rather, he is insisting that a faith-response to Jesus is only possible because his gracious, constant call empowers us to so reply. All are enabled by God's universal salvific will to respond — as best as can be done in each one's circumstances — to his offer of Life in Christ Jesus. "We love," says John, "because he first loved us " (1 Jn 4:19).

Faith and good works are not, then, opposed to each other; rather they are so intertwined that one cannot exist without the other. Faith is the root, the blossom is action.

Faith as *belief in a set of propositions* can in theory exist without love of God and neighbor. However, faith in its fullest sense — a personal response on every level of personality to the God who calls — includes love. Faith in its total meaning, as exemplified by Mary of the Annunciation, is vivified by love. And there is no love of God where there is no love of neighbor. "If anyone says, 'I love God,' but hates his brother, he is a liar; for he who does not love his brother whom he has seen, cannot love God whom he has not seen. And this commandment we have from God that he who loves God should love his brother also" (1 Jn 4:20-21). "By this shall all know that you are my disciples," says Jesus, "if you have love for one another" (Jn 13:35). Faith must always, then, be expressed in sincere and active love for one's neighbor.

The more intense our relationship to Jesus, the more alive and dynamic will be our life of service. There is no christian who apathetically stands aloof as most of the world goes to bed painfully hungry every night. No one can be called christian who yawns in disinterest as the evening news blares of discrimination, terrorism, flagrant acts of injustice. Enabled by the Spirit, the christian's faith necessarily entails involvement in the "joy and hope, the grief and anguish of people of our time, especially of those who are poor or afflicted in any way" (*Church in the Modern World*, 1).

This flowering of faith is not synonymous with feverish activity. For all, *prayer* in and for the Body of Christ is the primary apostolate. In the Heart of the Risen Jesus, the physical center of the cosmos, christians feed the hungry, clothe the naked, give drink to the thirsty, right injustice. In prayer through Christ and in Christ, the disciple touches with salvific healing the wounded of the world. The deeper our union with Christ the Head, the more intensely do we

23

share with the members of the Body of Christ. In contemplative prayer especially, we tug at the hem of the garment of Jesus and power goes out from him throughout the universe.

For most christians, this prayer is to be manifested in joyful, active, loving service to others. Like Saint Louis de Montfort, the majority of the followers of Jesus are called to be contemplatives *in action*, each according to his or her own vocation: the mother by her loving care for the family, the student by serious application to learning, the politician by publicly and fearlessly upholding gospel values, the pastor by total dedication to his parish. To the extent possible, all in this valley of tears must reach out to others in Christ. Faith calls us to feed the hungry, clothe the naked, give drink to the thirsty, instruct those who do not know the Lord. Faith must express itself in an overflow of love towards others; otherwise it is dead.

Mary, the model of contemplative union with her Son, so powerfully exemplifies the essential connection between true faith and service to neighbor. The second joyful mystery painted by Luke is the *Visitation* of Mary to her relative Saint Elizabeth. Here the rather complicated theological theories about the relationship of faith and active christian life are so simply and authentically clarified.

The distance between Nazareth and the hill country of Judah is fewer than a hundred miles. Not a long trip by today's standards but when donkey or camel were the principal means of transport, arduous and dangerous travel indeed. It is *with haste* that Mary undertakes this first missionary journey: the christian does not delay in caring for others, no matter the difficulties involved. In the Lucan portrait, *immediately upon surrendering to the Lord*, Mary expresses this faith in action. The apostolate, understood according to each one's vocation, is essential to faith. The young virgin mother of Nazareth, the new Ark of the Covenant —*the God-Bearer* —is sent into action by the Holy Spirit as the Old Testament Ark, the dwelling place of God, was carried into the battles of the Israelites as they triumphed over the Canaanites. The woman of faith is the first to proclaim the Lord, the first to conquer for Christ as she brings *Good News* to Elizabeth and John the Baptizer.

Luke does not tell us Mary's words of salutation to Elizabeth. He does underline, however, that through this greeting, God acts. It is *at the sound* of Mary's voice that John dances with joy in his mother's womb as David centuries before danced before the Ark (cf. 2 Sam 6). Evangelization takes place *through* the words of this woman of faith; the joy of God's presence is brought about *through* Mary's visit. Faith is being shared, God's healing presence is being experienced *through* Mary's voice. Through people of faith, God's power — omnipotent love — recreates this world, turning sorrow into dancing. Rightfully, Elizabeth exclaims, "Blessed is she who believed," for Mary, the woman of faith, has brought the rejoicing of the Savior to her home. So too all men and women of faith are *blessed*. Through them the power and joy of the Risen Lord is transforming all whom they meet.

The missionary journey of Mary as told by Luke concludes with the Canticle of Praise, the *Magnificat*. Perhaps the hymn has its principal source in the chants of early Jewish-christians; it may even echo a Maccabean war-cry. Nonetheless, it authentically clarifies the evangelical spirit of Mary and of all who follow the Lord. After every conquest for Christ, the christian must praise God, for *Holy is his Name*. He is the wellspring; faith is the sharing in his omnipotence. He is to be praised for sending the Spirit through the words and deeds of those who believe in him. We who are so *lowly*, of such *low estate*, must praise him for using us

25

as the active and responsible instruments of his glory. Praise of God, rejoicing in his goodness is an integral part of the apostolate. Often we have no inkling of what has been accomplished by our visit to the sick, our comfort to the bereaved, our instruction to those entering the church, our firm yet peaceful example of gospel values among those who scoff. No matter. We praise him, for *he who is mighty has done great things* for us and through us.

There is an aspect of the Visitation which although central, is often overlooked when considering faith in action. Mary, the model christian, cries out to God for the liberation of the poor, the hungry, the oppressed: "He has scattered the proud...he has put down the mighty...the rich he has sent empty away." But the poor, "he has filled with good things," he has "exalted" them.

The apostolate is not a passive, weak, fearful life. Rather, as we see in Mary, it is filled with the omnipotence of God, caught up in the front-lines of the battle, outspoken and bold in its *cry for the poor*. Mary typifies all christians who must by their very calling, be involved in the work for peace, justice and mercy. The second joyful mystery of the rosary reminds us that evangelization is not an option. It is an essential element of faith. Evangelization must include within it the faith-struggle for justice, for adequate clothing, food, shelter. *Redemption is not only of the soul but of the whole person*. Therefore, the faith-motivated struggle for justice for the oppressed, bread for the poor, healing of the ill, is not *pre-evangelization* but belongs to the proclamation of the Good News itself. The *Magnificat* sings that faith is liberating not only for oneself but for others also. To stand idly by as injustice, discrimination, hunger reign in this world is equivalent to denying the faith. Fearlessly, for God "remembers his mercy," and helps "his servants," the christian, like Mary, is a dynamic force in proclaiming to the world that Jesus is Lord. The follower of Jesus is, by loving voice and deed, the privileged instrument in carrying out the victory of our Lord Jesus Christ.

How often we have heard appeals to live our faith, to volunteer for service in the parish by visiting the sick, caring for the elderly, teaching the young. Yet many christians seem to be satisfied with *thinking* of those less fortunate. Some strangely calm a troubled conscience by feasting at luxurious banquets, "fund-raisers for the starving." Others assume they fulfill their privilege of discipleship by writing a perfunctory check for a charitable, non-profit organization. Is this the example of a *living* faith given to us by the Visitation Mary?

To the extent possible and in conformity with our vocation, christians must become "doers of the word" through active participation in the joys and sorrows of the world, especially of those around us. We must be ready to put our lives on the line to bring the Good News of Jesus to the poor, the lonely, the disenfranchised.

Such is the profound vision of faith taught us by our Lady of the Visitation, the second joyful mystery of the rosary.

May the grace of the mystery of the Visitation
come down into our hearts.

3
THE NATIVITY

A christian is counter-culture. Living the gospel values today is considered medieval, a sign of a backward mind. When with powerful prophetic voice, the church proclaims the lordship of Christ, economic and political justice, the inviolable value of human life, her words are scorned, ridiculed as an unwarranted interference. But the Good News of Jesus Christ is not an arid list of certitudes; it is a personal encounter with the enfleshed Wisdom of the Father resulting in a new vision of reality. The church is bound by the mandate of Christ himself to proclaim this Truth to the entire world no matter the results of Gallup polls or the threats of persecution. Blatantly, the First World countries especially reject the voice of the Body of Christ. Yet never can the church be passive as the crises of modern civilization crowd in upon humankind.

The church must, therefore, expect rejection. Did not the Lord himself tell us: "Behold, I send you out as sheep in the midst of wolves; so be wise as serpents and innocent as doves. Beware of men; for they will deliver you up to councils, and flog you in their synagogues and you will be dragged before governors and kings for my sake, to bear testimony before them and the Gentiles" (Mt 10:16-18). "Do not think that I have come to bring peace on earth; I have not come to bring peace but a sword...He who loves father or mother more than me is not worthy of me and he who loves son or daughter more than me is not worthy of me and he who does not take his cross and follow me is not worthy of me. He who finds his life will lose it and he who loses his life for my sake will find it" (Mt 10:34-39).

Rejection is a sign that the church is truly proclaiming

the gospel. When her confidants are the self-righteous mighty of this world, the church must ask herself if she is truly living and proclaiming the undiluted word of the Lord. The friends of Jesus were not the powerful leaders of the time but "tax collectors and sinners," the poor, the oppressed, the sick. They were *poor* for they were *open to his love.* It must be the same for the church as she proclaims the liberating message of the reign of God: her friends cannot be the oppressive economic, political cartel. Rather, the poor and rejected must find in the church their guardian and support and she must identify with them. The so-called "preferential option for the poor" is not an *option* at all; it is demanded by the gospel itself. It necessarily brings with it the scoffs and anger of the strong.

However, it is not an amorphous church which experiences rejection; it is the *individual christian* who at home, at the office, in school, in casual conversations at the supermarket, always is a living gospel of Jesus Christ. Few people ever examine the Scriptures; the christian must be, in word and action, the living gospel for all to read. Which means that in today's society, the faith-filled christian will surely know rejection.

It is Mary of the Nativity (Lk 2:1-20) who exemplifies this aspect of faith profoundly, poignantly. Obedient to the word, faithful to the will of God, she, the Ark of the Covenant carrying the New Law, is rejected at Bethlehem. "And she gave birth to her first-born son and wrapped him in swaddling clothes and laid him in a manger, *because there was no place for them in the inn*" (Lk 2:7). Mary had obeyed the word of God spoken through Gabriel, she had, although with difficulty, complied with the duty to be enrolled with Joseph at Bethlehem. Faithful to God's word, she now experiences rejection. The "inn," symbol of the pompous, worldly wise, rejects the woman bearing the New Covenant of Love. There is *no place in the inn* for the woman carrying Christ. Yet the poor—the shepherds—are, in the Lucan narrative, her friends.

There is no room, says the world boasting of its so-called independence from the "superstition of faith," for the christian proclaiming the gospel. Not that the christian *seeks* to be spurned! However, since the gospel does not mesh with worldly values, rejection comes as no surprise. Since fidelity to the teachings of the Body of Christ is mocked by a *do your own thing* generation, ridicule by the worldly-wise is integral to a life of faith. It is the applause of Christ the christian values, not the plaudits of the world.

Mary of the Nativity, homeless, rejected, is the sign of the cost of discipleship. She exemplifies the words of her Son who tells us that persecution is integral to following him (cf. Mk 10:30). Faith entails rejection by the haughty and the proud, by the "inns" of contemporary society.

Where does Mary find the strength to continue? As the mystery of her Son begins ever so slowly to unravel, her faith is surely tempted. The rejection at Bethlehem is but the first, she may well surmise, of future even more painful refusals. How often does a Catholic, ridiculed for obedience to the church, wonder how long he or she can bear under the increasing peer-pressure to reject the faith? Mary of the Nativity discloses the secret of perseverance in spite of rejection.

It easily goes unnoticed that Mary is given another *name* in the Nativity scene: "the pondering woman" (cf Lk 2:19). Reflecting on the message of the Angels as narrated by the shepherds, recalling the rejection by the "inn," the birth of the beautiful Child, "she kept all these things, pondering them in her heart." The word *pondering* implies a futile attempt to "put the pieces together." There is no way that she can "make sense" of what has happened, no way that she, of herself, can be strong enough to face the evidently painful future. All she can do is to gaze lovingly at the Christ Child, in wonderment, in praise. She is "the pondering one," she is the *contemplative* woman. The pieces do not fit; she can only stare in amazement at this Child, the "Son of the Most High" (Lk 1:32). Contemplative prayer, which typifies Mary, is the source of her strength to be faithful in spite of rejection, to be obedient in spite of the jibes and scoffing which will inevitably be hers as the mother of the Lord.

The Holy Spirit is emphatically teaching us that it is impossible to live the christian faith in the midst of this world unless we are contemplatives. We too must be *ponderers* of the Word. Faith can only be sustained by intimate, loving discourse with God. Daily, we must "waste time" with the Lord so that we may be filled with the joyful strength to be proclaimers of the Word. Since faith is a living relationship with the Lord, prayer becomes an absolute necessity for a disciple of Jesus; relationships weaken and may even die without regular communication. Through meditative reading of his word, through the eucharistic sacrifice, through daily gazing at the Lord, through the contemplative recitation of the rosary, the followers of Christ find the strength to radiate the gospel in spite of ridicule and rejection.

Rejected by the "inn" because of her obedience of faith, Mary of the Nativity remains faithful by "pondering these things in her heart." She is the example for all christians. Living in the atmosphere of Mary as Saint Louis de Montfort advocates, following her example, open to her maternal influence, the modern christian finds the divine energy to be — in spite of rejection by the world's standards — the living proclamation that Jesus Christ is Lord!

May the grace of the mystery of the Nativity
come down into our hearts.

31

4
THE PRESENTATION

What is faith? Theologians dispute the answer, the question befuddles the ordinary christian. Faith is too broad a topic, too profound, too deeply rooted in our lives to be adequately expressed in words. The joyful mysteries respond to this central issue of christianity by painting a magnificent portrait of the model disciple, Mary. In her, we see faith *lived.*

The Annunciation presents Mary, empowered by the Spirit, totally surrendering to God on every level of her personality: the very root of faith.

The Visitation describes the mother of the Lord as the missionary, the evangelizer: an intrinsic element of faith.

The Nativity depicts Mary as the woman carrying Jesus yet spurned by the "inn" — symbol of the world — and only through prayer remaining faithful in spite of rejection: a consequence of faith.

It is *the Presentation* (Lk 2:22-40), the fourth joyful mystery, which emphasizes a facet of faith which contemporary christians tend to overlook: faith is *obedience* which brings about a sharing in the sufferings of the Lord.

Obedience is a synonym for faith. In his **Letter to the Romans**, the Apostle of the Gentiles speaks about "the obedience of faith " (Rom 16:26) for both faith and obedience essentially mean being in harmonious relationship. Since it is God who calls us to this all-encompassing new life with him, it can only be sustained by remaining in accord with his will. It can only be kept alive through a total, loving, active and responsible surrender to his mysterious ways: the definition of obedience. "If you love me," says Jesus, "keep my commandments" (Jn 14:15). There is no faith in the full sense of the term where there is disobedience. There is no faith where the creature is out of harmony with the Creator.

When Jesus commands: "Follow me!" he leaves no room for picking and choosing what we — on our own — believe suits us best. He alone is "the way, the truth and the life." Obedience and faith go hand in hand.

This conformity to God's will requires living the gospel-demands no matter the cost. It comprises an assent "of will and mind" to the Spirit of Truth as He speaks to us through his Body, the church, the "pillar and ground of truth" (1 Tim 3:15; cf. Second Vatican Council, **Constitution on the Church**, no.25). A knowing and willing defiance of the word of God, rebellion against his Body, the church, shatters our loving relationship with the Lord. Where there is no obedience, there is no faith.

It appears that Luke is intent on getting this message across in the opening pages of his gospel. Since he is proclaiming Jesus as "Savior who is Christ the Lord," (Lk 2:11) the evangelist tells us that we must be obedient to this word if it is to recreate us into the image of the Son of God. Luke explains this obedience of faith by presenting Mary as the faith-filled - the obedient - woman. It is strongly accentuated in the Presentation narrative.

Scripture tells us that Mary and Joseph bring the Infant Jesus to Jerusalem to present him to the Lord, for this is, as the gospel underlines, "according to the law of Moses" (v.22). The evangelist insists upon this obedience when he repeats that the Presentation of the Child Jesus is an act of observance of the Law: the parents offer a sacrifice "according to what is said in the law of the Lord " (v.24) and "the parents brought in the child Jesus to do for him according to the custom of the law" (v.27). No less than five times (vv. 22, 23, 24, 27, 39) Luke highlights that the observances were carried out according to the law. The obedience of Mary becomes even more apparent for it can well be presumed that - according to the Lucan scenario - she could consider herself exempt from any need of "purification" for her conception of the Child was virginal; moreover, why should Jesus, already described by Luke as "the Lord," need to be "redeemed" by an offering? Yet that total surrender of faith - which is the very characteristic of Mary - exemplifies itself in her total obedience, observing "the law of the Lord."

It is only within the context of the strength of Mary's obedience of faith that we should consider the best known scene of the Presentation narrative, Simeon's prophecy that Mary's soul will be pierced: "And Simeon blessed them and said to Mary his mother, 'Behold, this child is set for the fall and rising of many in Israel and for a sign that is spoken against (and a sword will pierce through your own soul also) that thoughts out of many hearts may be revealed' " (vv. 34-35).

Faith is a sharing-with. Mary, through her obedience of faith shares in the life of her Son and, therefore, shares in his obedience to the Father which leads him to the cross. Mary's faith will bring her so intimately, so deeply into the sufferings of her Son. In the fourth joyful mystery, she obediently - and with maternal anguish - presents her Redeemer Son to the Father in our name. It is her faith which makes her *Our Lady of Sorrows.*

All who share with Christ in his "rising" can only do so by sharing in his "falling" in death upon the cross. Paul expresses this beautifully in his letter to the Philippians: "that I may know him and the power of his resurrection and may share his sufferings, becoming like him in his death that if possible, I may attain the resurrection from the dead" (3:10-11). The cross is intrinsic to a life of faith. Since no one is more obedient to Christ than Mary his mother, no one shares so deeply in his sufferings; no one shares so fully in the "falling" (the sufferings) and the "rising" (the resurrection) of Jesus.

Mary teaches us that suffering - sharing in the cross of Christ - is intrinsic to a christian life. The Risen Lord himself told the disciples on the road to Emmaus: "Was it not necessary that the Christ should suffer these things and so enter into his glory?" (Lk 24:26). The same holds for the follower of Christ. It is only by denying oneself, taking up the cross, that we can share in the glory of the Risen Lord (cf. Mk 8:34), it is only by dying that the grain of wheat can sprout in newness of life (cf. Jn 12:24). There is no shortcut to the empty tomb: the only path goes over Calvary's hill. Easter does not come after Good Friday; the resurrection does not take place after death on the cross. Rather, it is through the cross that Jesus enters into his glory, it is only through suffering that we share in the glory of Christ's resurrection. Eternal life does not come after death; rather, it is only through death that we share in the eternal victory of the Lord. It is only through the falling that we share in the rising: "this child is set for the fall and the rising of many in Israel" (Lk 2:34).

Like Mary, all the disciples of Christ must experience "fall and rising" - all must share in the cross in order to know the glory of the Risen Lord. No wonder that Saint Louis de Montfort had such a love for the cross! Participating in Mary's faith, he knows that obedience to the Lord necessarily means embracing his cross and through the cross, sharing in omnipotent Love who is God.

Mary of the Presentation tells us that a christianity which strips suffering from a follower of Christ is an unrecognizable caricature. Suffering - the cross - is intrinsic to anyone who obeys Jesus' command, "Follow me!" Since faith is a sharing-with, the christian must participate in the cross of Christ who turns our weaknesses and sins into victory by the glorious cross.

It is this Spirit-filled insight into suffering - no matter the kind - that enables us to say with Saint Louis de Montfort,

"What a cross to be without a cross!" Through the cross we arrive at the empty tomb and encounter the Risen Christ. Through the cross we share in the victory of the Redeemer. The obedience of faith plunges us into Christ Crucified enabling us to share in the glory of the Resurrection.

Such is the profound vision of faith given to us by the Lucan narrative of the fourth joyful mystery of the rosary. Simeon's prophecy already gives us a glimpse of the sorrowful mysteries to come.

May the grace of the mystery of the Presentation in the Temple come down into our hearts.

5

THE FINDING IN THE TEMPLE

Have you ever *lost* Jesus? Are there times when the Lord seems *absent*, deaf to your cries, blind to your needs? As stormy as such experience is, it is intrinsic to authentic faith! Any mature christian knows those days of total emptiness when we ask and do not receive, knock yet no one opens, search but find nothing. Or at least so it appears.

All experience at various times this "losing of Jesus" or as the mystics term it, *the dark night of the soul*. It is intrinsic to a dynamic life of faith. The mother mourning the death of her infant, the husband caught up in a devastating divorce, the monk stripped of any sense of accomplishment, the desertion of a friend, an incurable illness, an apparent defeat, or just an indefinable spiritual malaise - all can trigger such a radical "self-emptying" that we find ourselves in that phase of growth in faith which can be called "the loss of Jesus." In the midst of turmoil and dryness, he seems nowhere to be found. It is not that the tide of his love seems low; rather the ocean itself has vanished. This almost unbearable sharing in the dark night - intrinsic to our life in the crucified and risen Christ - may be the occasion for a new depth of union with the Lord. It can also make us prey to discouragement, depression, anger, inclining many to turn their back on faith itself.

Before Luke narrates the public ministry of Jesus, he describes the essentials entailed in following Christ. He does this through the joyful, colorful pageant of the infancy narrative. One of the principal characters in this authentic "play" is Mary, the mother of Jesus. In the five scenes in which she appears, we see faith as lived by this first christian, this first disciple of the Lord. It is in the final scene, *The Finding of Jesus in the Temple* that Mary so beautifully fulfills the role of the woman of faith who *loses Jesus.* Through her example, the evangelist tells us how to deepen our faith through this terrifying yet fruitful experience of the *dark night of the soul.*

Luke, the inspired master playwright, relates that Mary and Joseph *lose Jesus* on the return trip from Jerusalem. As part of the caravan of relatives, friends and neighbors who had gone up to the Holy City for the Passover, they thought that Jesus was with another section of the large group. (How often a mother, returning from a neighborhood outing is sure that her youngster is in the other bus!) The approximately eighty mile journey was only in its first day when Mary and Joseph sought out their Child. He was nowhere to be found. No one has seen him. The joy of his presence suddenly gone. Jesus is lost.

Leaving the security of the caravan, they return to Jerusalem in an intense search of their child. Luke describes this period as *three days,* anticipating the desolating emptiness of that final (so the disciples believed!) loss of Jesus from Good Friday to Easter morn. Guilt feelings, upset, questioning, all are the innuendoes of this dramatic Lucan scene. The child Jesus, so mysterious yet so ordinary, is he lost forever? Is this part of God's plan? It is here that Luke gives us - through the first disciple, Mary -indicators of how we are to act when our life of faith is in the same situation, when we too *lose Jesus.*

First, we must never let discouragement overwhelm us. In spite of all the conflicting emotions boiling over within them, Mary and Joseph continue to seek their Child, to live their faith. This implies not only hope but more fundamentally, a conviction that - against all appearance - they *are* loved by God. The pitch black darkness is the infinite brightness of his Love permeating us, blinding us. Mary continues to trust in God *even though she does not understand what is happening.* Here we have the most fundamental attitude of faith in the midst of trial: total and often painful surrender to God's inscrutable love.

38

When Jesus is found, Mary gives vent to the anguish and hurt she experienced because of the loss of her Child: "Son, why have you treated us so? Behold, your father and I have been looking for you anxiously" (Lk 2:48). The first christian speaks the words which will be on the lips of all sincere followers of Jesus: "Lord, why??" And like Mary, we do not understand the reply, we cannot grasp the reason why. Yet with Mary, in spite of the devastating loss, we must remain faithful, trusting in his love.

It is this firm conviction of being loved which saves us not only from disabling discouragement but also impels us to pray even during the *darkness of the night.* Is this, perhaps, what Luke is teaching us when he tells us that Mary and Joseph sought the child *in the temple?* May we not presume that this Lucan drama is advising us to enter into the House of God, to immerse ourselves in the wordless prayer of total abandonment especially when *the loss of Jesus* is so acute? In this final scene of the infancy narrative, Luke foreshadows that final scene of the Lord's public ministry, his death on Calvary. When we experience this loss, the Spirit tells us that our primary attitude must be one of hope and prayerful trust, following the example of Mary.

And this brings Luke to the second fundamental attitude when we too *lose Jesus.* We must be convinced that this stripping of self, this emptiness of self, is but a preparation for a new fullness of glory. It is *on the third day* that Jesus is found, which appears to have a double connotation: the dark night is of a length of time which *we* cannot determine and its end result — provided we are faithful — will be a more intense union with the Risen Lord. It is the resurrection through the cross, Easter through Calvary, light through darkness. Intrinsic to a life of faith is the conviction that the ultimate outcome is victory! Because of the resurrection, the goal of the entire universe is already in place, the *final* chapter already published: "Thanks be to God who gives us the victory through our Lord Jesus Christ!" (1 Cor 15:57). This episode of the dark night, of the *loss of Jesus* is also swallowed up in this certain victory of Christ. It is this conviction that enables us to be firm in the faith even when the darkness urges us to desert.

This victorious outcome of the *loss of Jesus* is expressed in the Lucan narrative in powerful terms: "And he went down with them and came to Nazareth and was obedient to them." Jesus the Lord, the personal manifestation of the Wisdom of the Father, obeys our wishes! He whom the winds and the sea obey (cf Mk 4:41) obeys his creatures. This final aspect of faith in this Lucan drama is the most spectacular of all: Faith is a *sharing-with*. God shares our weakness so that we may share his omnipotence. Jesus accepts our total surrender so that He may truly be our servant (cf Mk 10:45). The first scene in which Mary appears in the Lucan infancy narrative sees Mary expressing her obedience to the Lord: "Behold the handmaid of the Lord, be it done to me according to thy word" (Lk 1:38). The final act concludes with the obedience of Jesus to his faithful disciples: and he "was obedient to them."

The *loss of Jesus*, this *dark night*, endured with loving, prayerful hope, ends up in the glory of new life with the victorious Lord: the lesson taught us by the woman of faith who *loses Jesus*.

The Lucan overture ends. The final curtain falls on this pageant of faith outlined in his first two chapters. The joyful mysteries of the rosary are complete. Through Mary, the first disciple, we now know how we are to hear the word of God, we understand what it means to follow Jesus, we have been taught the mystery of faith. Luke can now begin his proclamation of the public ministry of Jesus, Son of Mary.

May the grace of the Finding in the Temple
come down into our hearts.

The Sorrowful Mysteries
INTRODUCTION

Have you ever noticed that the rosary completely omits meditations on the *ministry* of Jesus? The *joyful* mysteries contemplate the infancy narratives of Luke, the *sorrowful* bring us to the passion and death of Jesus, the *glorious* praise the exaltation of the Risen Lord and of his Body, the church. The fifteen meditations which comprise the rosary do not include the Lord's baptism, his itinerant proclamation of the Good News of the kingdom first in Galilee and then in Judea; they have no mention of the transfiguration, of his powerful miracles, beautiful sermons, challenging parables. The official rosary mysteries skip over the public ministry of Jesus.

Not exactly correct. The rosary *presupposes* the public ministry of Jesus as it begins the sorrowful mysteries, much like the first christians *presupposed* the public ministry when they preached the victorious passion and death of the Lord.

It appears that the early church, in the progressive development of its proclamation of Jesus, *first* formulated the passion narrative. This is the core of the gospel. What may well be the earliest catechism lesson of the first christians begins with this truth: "Christ died for our sins in accordance with the Scriptures..." (1 Cor 15:3). The sermons of Peter in Luke's *Acts of the Apostles* stress this central belief of all christians: "Let all the house of Israel therefore know assuredly that God has made him both Lord and Christ, this Jesus whom you crucified" (2:36). The triumphant cross summarized the preaching of the first followers of Jesus.

41

Were the early christians skipping over the public ministry of Jesus? Not really. For not only will it become explicitly formulated in the preaching of the Good News, but it is always *presupposed* whenever the triumphant cross is proclaimed. Peter makes this clear in his first sermon in Jerusalem, preaching Christ crucified and risen: "Men of Israel, hear these words: Jesus of Nazareth, a man attested to you by God with mighty works and wonders and signs which God did through him in your midst, as you yourselves know..." (Acts 2:22)

The second series of rosary mysteries *presupposes* the public ministry of Jesus. This Jesus whom we contemplate suffering and dying for us is the One who proclaimed Good News of peace "throughout all Judea, beginning from Galilee after the baptism which John preached: ...God anointed Jesus of Nazareth with the Holy Spirit and with power; ...he went about doing good and healing all that were oppressed by the devil, for God was with him" (Acts 10:37-38). As Peter does not enter into the details of Christ's years of public ministry but quickly summarizing them, preaches that "they put him to death by hanging him on a tree" (Acts 10:39), so too the rosary mysteries presuppose the events and words of Jesus' public life as it contemplates the Passion of Jesus the Lord.

In praying the rosary, we need not only *presume* the public life of Jesus. Saint Louis de Montfort's fourth method of saying the rosary *(God Alone, The Collected Writings of Saint Louis Marie de Montfort,* pp. 243-251) dedicates nine of the ten *Hail Mary's* of the fifth joyful mystery to an explicit meditation on aspects of the public ministry such as the miracles of Jesus, his transfiguration, the institution of the eucharist, etc.

Mary's characteristics of faith - shared with us through the *joyful* mysteries - must accompany us through the *sorrowful.* Through the vibrant faith of the first christian, Mary, we gaze at our Lord betrayed, scourged, crowned with thorns, carrying the cross, crucified. Her influence will enable us to see our suffering crucified Lord more clearly, to love him more dearly, to be united with him more immediately and intensely.

The cross is evidently the theme of the sorrowful mysteries. The topic, as Paul strongly notes, the great "stumbling-block" in evangelization (cf 1 Cor 1:23). Why? We preach Christ *crucified*, a Messiah who undergoes the worst execution that the depraved mind could invent. We boldly declare that this Christ is truly the Son of God. It is beyond the capabilities of the human psyche to invent a God who "so loved the world that he gave his only Son" (cf Jn 3:16) to suffer and die *for us*.

At the root, then, of the mystery of the cross is the infinite, unmerited, unconditional love that God has for us. To be more precise, God does not *have* love for us, as if love were a characteristic which God *at times* possesses. Not at all. God *is* Love and therefore God can only *be* Love and can only love us. Sin is its own punishment and draws us out of the infinite Light who is God. But the Light is always on. We are the ones who freely walk into the darkness when committing deadly sin. By contemplating the cross, we know that we are loved and always empowered to return to the infinite Light radiating from the pierced Heart of Christ.

The sorrowful mysteries of the rosary presume that we accept that we are accepted, that we rejoice in being loved infinitely and unconditionally by Love itself; otherwise, the mystery of the cross is nothing more than folly. At the same time, meditating on these mysteries we come to a deeper experience of Christ crucified, of being embraced by infinite Love. Through the power of the Holy Spirit, the sorrowful mysteries enable us to "understand" that God yearns for us more than we can ever desire God.

43

Finally, the sorrowful mysteries shed some light on our own sufferings. The passion and death of our Savior reveal the radical depths of the sin of the world, the brokenness of the cosmos, the estrangement which so characterizes human existence, for we creatures have crucified our incarnate Creator. It is evident to all that we have not as yet fully implemented the victory of the triumphant cross. We are still "of little faith." Caught up in this radical disharmony, we are not only in the crossfire of the conflict between the victorious cross and rebellious humanity but we also contribute to the battle by our personal sins. Even the most innocent, a child in the womb, is affected by this world not fully turned to the redemptive cross. Abortion, the murder of the innocents, is not punishment inflicted on the unborn child who is, moreover, incapable of sinning. It is in itself a heinous sin of members of the human family which has not yet fully accepted the victory of the cross, a family which has not agreed by faith to the peace won by our crucified Brother.

Yet the cross also shows us the value of suffering. Although an evil in itself, suffering becomes a healing medicine for this world when joined with the crucified Jesus. To love our God even when suffering is so acute has a ripple effect throughout the universe, slowly calming the rebellion. To love in the midst of suffering is an effect of meditating on the sorrowful mysteries. It is as if God grants us a new vision enabling us to "understand" the divine mystery that it is *only* by sharing in Christ's cross that we come to the resurrection. "Make no mistake about it," says Saint Louis de Montfort, "since incarnate Wisdom had to enter heaven by the cross, you also must enter by the same way" *(Love of the Eternal Wisdom,* 180). It is *only* through the sorrowful mysteries that we arrive at the glorious. Since Saint Louis de Montfort lived the mystery of the cross so joyfully and preached it so eloquently, his teachings will guide us as we examine this second set of rosary mysteries.

With Mary, the mother of the crucified Savior, we now contemplate the core of the gospel, the triumphant cross, the sorrowful mysteries of the rosary.

1

THE AGONY IN THE GARDEN

Breathing the calm atmosphere flowing from the soft music of *Hail Mary's,* we enter into the first sorrowful mystery of the rosary, the *Agony in the Garden.*

This first meditation is better understood in the context of the Last Supper, a method recommended by Saint Louis de Montfort. John's gospel reveals an extraordinary event which takes place during this *Farewell Meal* with his apostles:

> "And during supper, when the devil had already put it into the heart of Judas Iscariot, Simon's son, to betray him, Jesus, knowing that the Father had given all things into his hands and that he had come from God and was going to God, rose from supper, laid aside his garments and girded himself with a towel. Then he poured water into a basin and began to wash the disciples' feet and to wipe them with the towel with which he was girded" (Jn 13:2-5).

Like all the fellowship meals of Jesus with the poor, the outcast, the despised, the Last Supper especially is an effective sign of *a covenant of love* which Jesus makes with his rebellious human family. Jesus, especially at this final meal, yearns to intensify his relationship of love with us. Therefore, like the prophets of old he carries out a symbolic act which more intensely brings about and reveals the reality of his existence. Washing the feet of his disciples, he demonstrates the essence of his life: he is our servant, or more precisely, our slave. He is *for us.* In fact, when Peter protests: "You shall never wash my feet." Jesus firmly declares that if Simon Peter refuses to permit Jesus to serve him, the apostle will have "no part in me" (Jn 13:8). To enter the kingdom, we must permit the Son of God to be our servant.

Jesus is *for us*. God in Christ reveals that from all eternity he has freely willed to be *for us*. The most touching words of the entire Bible are found in Isaiah where Yahweh tells us: "Can a mother forget her suckling child, that she should have no compassion on the son of her womb? Even these may forget, yet I will never forget you." Perhaps alluding to the mark of a slave, Yahweh astoundingly declares: "Behold, I have carved you on the palms of my hands" (49:15-16). God is ours. He is *for us*.

Jesus is the Incarnation of this infinite Love *for us*. In the gospel of Mark, Jesus tells us that "the son of man has come not to be served but to serve and to give his life as a ransom for all" (10:45). In Luke, Jesus tells us: "For which is the greater, the one who sits at table or the one who serves? Is it not the one who sits at table? But I am among you as one who serves" (22:27). At the Last Supper, before proceeding to the Mount of Olives, not only does Jesus demonstrate that he is our servant by washing the feet of the disciples, but taking a loaf of bread, solemnly pronounces the eucharistic words changing the bread into his body, *for us*. The cup of wine becomes the new covenant in his blood, *poured out for us* (cf Lk 22:20; 1 Cor 11:25; Mk 14:24; Mt 26:26-28).

Immediately after this final supper with his disciples, Jesus, having again revealed his being as Love *for us*, goes to his customary place of prayer, a grove of olive trees on the mount overlooking Jerusalem. The agony in the garden reveals the anguish and fear of Jesus in fulfilling his very being: the infinite Wisdom of the Father who takes on the form of a slave, obedient even unto death, even death upon the cross, *for us*.

The first sorrowful mystery is found, with some variations, in Mark and the two gospels which depend upon him, Matthew and Luke: Mk 14:32-42; Lk 22:39-46; Mt 26:36-46. John's gospel omits this episode entirely.

The agony in the garden is the beginning of the passion of our Lord Jesus Christ. The suffering of our Lord in this first sorrowful mystery is beyond the power of the human mind to grasp.

Often Jesus had gone to Gethsemani, the Mount of Olives. There he and his disciples would rest or Jesus would spend the night in prayer. Judas, one of the Twelve, knew the place well. For hours Jesus prayed to his Father while the disciples, not fully understanding that the "hour of darkness" had arrived, fell soundly asleep.

We can well imagine that as Jesus prayed, he looked across the narrow Kidron valley into the Temple area. From the Roman fortress — the *Antonia* — situated at the north-west corner of the Temple esplanade, lanterns of soldiers began to file out into the darkness. Once outside the city walls, the column headed for the olive grove. Jesus knew that the police were now coming to arrest him.

Falling prostrate on the ground, he begged the Father: "Let this cup pass from me!" Nowhere in the gospels is the humanity of the Lord so evident as here. Nowhere in the scriptural portraits does Jesus express such agonizing terror of suffering, such deep anguish and distress as he is about to fulfill his destiny: to offer his life in love to the Father, *for us.* Trembling with fear, drenched with the sweat of agony, he watches the torches coming up the hill towards him. Judas — one of his closest followers — is at the head of the contingent.

Run away? Would it not have been possible in the darkness of the night? But from the depths of his being, he cries out: "ABBA!" The word of a child for its own father. A babbling sound of tender love, of firm obedience. "ABBA, Father, all things are possible to thee; remove this cup from me; yet not what I will but what thou wilt" (Mk 14:36). To run away would be to betray his very self, to betray the mission given him by the Father to proclaim the reign of God. At the beginning of his ministry he boldly announced: "I must proclaim the kingdom of God...for I was sent for this purpose" (Lk 4:43). His fidelity would be expressed in obedience "unto death, even death upon a cross" (Phil 2:8).

The intensity of Jesus' agony in the garden is only understood in the context of his betrayal. Suffering supported by a loving, sharing community becomes mysteriously endurable. If loneliness and betrayal are joined to suffering, it becomes a taste of hell. And this Jesus suffered. Luke alone adds the presence of a comforting angel to the agony account (although the oldest Lucan manuscript omits it).

The traitor, incredibly, is one of the Twelve. A kiss, the sign of love, consummates the betrayal: "Is it with a kiss, Judas, that you hand over the Son of Man?" (Lk 22:48). Both Matthew and Luke speak not only of the sleep of the disciples during Jesus' agony but add that at the arrest, "they all forsook him and fled" (Mk 14:50; Mt 26:56). Mark heightens this desertion of Jesus with the story of the young man who followed Jesus at the arrest but when seized by the police, runs away naked (Mk 14:51-52). In *The Love of the Eternal Wisdom*, Saint Louis de Montfort summarizes this pain of betrayal: "He suffered in his disciples, one of whom bartered him for money and betrayed him; another, their leader, denied him, and the rest abandoned him" (159).

Alone, Jesus faces trial and condemnation. Peter follows but only at a safe distance (Lk 22:54), apparently afraid of being arrested along with Jesus. In utter loneliness, Jesus, the Lord of glory, is led away to his trial. The eternal and incarnate Wisdom, the human face of God, infinite Love incarnate, is seized like a common criminal to be judged by his creatures. For our sins and for our salvation, he is "led like a sheep to the slaughter" (Is 53:7).

Where is Mary during this agony and arrest of her Son?

From all eternity, God freely wills to externalize his Word *as the Son of Mary*. It is, then, utterly impossible, according to the Father's plan of salvation, to separate the mother from the Son: Jesus is forever the fruit of her faith. Our Lady is, therefore, "the inseparable companion of his life, of his death,..." (*True Devotion*, 74). Who can ever dare explain the connatural relationship of knowledge and love which unites every mother and child? Who can, then, understand the union of Mary with Jesus, especially when she sees that he is being hunted down, that his arrest is near? She was not with him physically in the *Agony in the Garden*. She was present far more intimately. She was with him as mother. "Not where I breathe, but where I love, I live" says the poet, Robert Southwell. The love which unites mother and Son is beyond comprehension and especially so as the passion begins.

The news of Jesus' impending arrest by the authorities has surely reached Mary. She knows the tortures inflicted on "criminals." The mother is more united to her Son than all the disciples. Who can begin to grasp the sufferings she endures as her Son enters into the final drama of his life, his ignominious death upon the cross?

It is within the suffering heart of Mary that we meditate on the *Agony in the Garden*. It is with her that we contemplate our Blessed Lord "who in the days of his flesh offered prayers and supplications with loud cries and tears, to him who was able to save him from death..." (Heb 5:7).

May the grace of the mystery of the Agony in the Garden come down into our hearts.

2

THE SCOURGING AT THE PILLAR

The **Scourging at the Pillar**, is, in a certain sense, the summary of these sorrowful meditations of the rosary. It is the consequence of the ultimate rejection of Jesus by his own and of the condemnation of Jesus by the Roman authorities; moreover, it is for Jesus' executioners, the beginning of the crucifixion of the Lord of glory. To gaze at Jesus being scourged by the Roman soldiers is to contemplate, as in resume, the horrendous sufferings of Christ.

Saint Louis de Montfort includes the *Trial Scene* and the *Denial of Jesus by Peter* within this decade of the rosary. Rightly so, for Mark only speaks of the scourging after the trial presided by the "chief priests and the council" (Mk 14: 53-65) and after the interrogation by Pilate which led to the release of Barabbas.

The second sorrowful mystery comprises, therefore, a contemplation of Jesus rejected by his own, infinite Love spurned by his creatures. The mystery has four scenes: the trial of Jesus, the denial by Peter, the crowd's preference for Barabbas over Jesus, and then as a culmination, the horrible scourging at the pillar.

The precise chronology and phases of the trial scene are impossible to reconstruct. The gospels have a far more momentous purpose than the mere rattling off of facts and figures. They present to us the Spirit-inspired interpretation of these events so that we may be caught up in the salvific love of Christ.

The trial before the Council (the *Sanhedrin*) describes the incredible rejection of Jesus by his own. The corrupt leaders of the time are determined to kill the incarnate Beloved, the Wisdom of God who freely has entered into the family to bring the light of life. Creatures judge the Creator. And the creatures "condemned him as deserving death" (Mk 14:64). The recitation of the rosary is the time to let this horrendous truth challenge us, interpret us, interrogate us. Immersed in this mystery, we are engulfed by the gravity of sin and specifically of our own sinfulness. Sin is the refusal to be loved by Love itself. It entails denying our reality as creatures and in our destructive self-centeredness and pride, act as if we are the norm, we are our own goal, we are the ones to determine what is right and what is wrong. How often do we repeat the sin of Adam and Eve! The haughtiness of the Council and its abominable condemnation of Jesus reflect ourselves.

In a certain sense, we are far more responsible than the members of the Sanhedrin. For God had literally surprised them by the mystery of the Incarnation. "God will visit his people," was always their belief. But that the very Wisdom of God would be personally manifest as a poor, unlettered vagabond from the despised northern part of the country, from a town so insignificant that it is not even mentioned in the Old Testament, was far beyond what they expected or could endure. And this Jesus proclaims himself as the *reign of Yahweh!*

We are more fortunate. We encounter the risen Christ in the sacraments, we hear his words in scripture as proclaimed by the pillar and ground of truth, the church, we experience the power of the gospel in our daily lives, we know of the maternal care of Our Lady. Yet, we regularly put Jesus on trial when things do not appear to go *our* way and how often we condemn him by turning to ourselves or to others as idols. How specifically each person does this, only the depth of one's conscience can say.

Peter's denial of Jesus three times typifies this. The impulsive, bravado leader of the apostles manages to get "right into the courtyard of the high priest" (Mk 14:54). Accused by the bystanders of being a follower of Jesus, Peter angrily curses back: "I do not know this man of whom you speak" (Mk 14:71). Betrayed by Judas, denied by Peter, deserted by the other apostles, Jesus faces torture and execution, alone. God — who in himself is perfection, needing no one or no thing — never chooses to leave his creation alone even when it brazenly rebels. Creation — which has an absolute need of God for its very existence — chooses not only to desert its Source but to condemn it. The disharmony of sin is now total discordance, absolute cacophony. Yet in the midst of the pandemonium, infinite Love incarnate will cry out from the cross: "Father, forgive them, for they know not what they do" (Lk 23:34). The second sorrowful mystery enters into the deepest recesses of the human heart and discovers in the midst of personal terrifying sin, the infinitely more powerful forgiveness of God.

"So Pilate, wishing to satisfy the crowd, released for them Barabbas; and having scourged Jesus, he delivered him to be crucified" (Mk 15:15; cf Lk 23:18; Jn 18:40). The scourging, then, came after the incredible decision of the mob to have Jesus crucified and Barabbas released.

Who was this Barabbas? The Scriptures only tell us that he was "a rebel who had committed murder in the insurrection." The contrast is between a murderer, a rebel, and the **Prince of Peace**. However, the comparison is even more striking: *Barabbas* in Aramaic means "Son of the father." In some ancient manuscripts, he is called *Jesus* Barabbas which is not too surprising since *Jesus* or its equivalent, *Joshua*, was not an uncommon name in New Testament times. The choice is then between Jesus the son of the father, and Jesus the Son of God the Father. The mob intercedes for Barabbas but refuses to do so for the eternal and incarnate Wisdom, Jesus. How often sin poses under the guise of good! The mob can pride itself on freeing a criminal so that it may condemn the Holy One of God.

The gospel is telling us that we have a decision to make, a determination which is constantly before us: to accept or reject Jesus the Lord. Like all the saints, Louis de Montfort reminds us that *we* are the ones who constantly choose Barabbas over Christ by our sins. Perhaps it is because of our fearful silence in the midst of a world screaming condemnation of gospel values that we are most seriously guilty.

The condemnation of Jesus to the horrible execution by crucifixion is done by order of Pilate whom the Romans themselves considered an inflexible, merciless and obstinate man, continually given to corruption, violence and cruelty of every kind. The King of glory, the Judge of the living and the dead, stands before Caesar's puppet and is condemned to die a criminal's execution. The creature condemns the Creator; the sinner crucifies the Holy One; the folly of this world executes the eternal and incarnate Wisdom. Never has this creation witnessed such a distortion, the climactic point of the sin of the world.

The crucifixion begins with the scourging at the pillar. Through the writings of Josephus, a Jewish historian of the first century, it is clear that this most terrible punishment was the normal prelude to crucifixion. The criminal, often stripped and bound to a pillar, was beaten repeatedly with knotted leather whips loaded with bone or metal so that the body could literally be torn apart. Scourging as a preliminary to crucifixion would continue until the flesh itself was exposed, lacerated, bleeding. However, care would be taken so that the prisoner would not be killed by the whippings in order that he may undergo the sufferings of hanging on a cross.

Jesus, our God in a fully human way, is beaten, scourged, spit upon. It is only when we gaze at Jesus close to dying by the scourging at the pillar, that we begin to understand the enormity of sin and even more so, the infinity of God's love.

As we contemplate Jesus scourged, torn, betrayed, we know that God in Jesus Christ can truly sympathize with us no matter how horrible the situation. "For we have not a high priest who is unable to sympathize with our weaknesses but one who in every respect has been tempted as we are, yet without sinning...He can deal gently with the ignorant and the wayward since he himself is beset with weakness...Let us with confidence draw near to the throne of grace that we may receive mercy and find his grace to help in time of need" (Heb 4:15; 5:2; 4:16).

As we contemplate Jesus literally torn from head to foot, we see fulfilled the tragic poem of the prophet Isaiah:

"He had no form or comeliness that we should look at him, and no beauty that we should desire him.

He was despised and rejected by men; a man of sorrows and acquainted with grief;

And as one from whom men hide their faces he was despised and we esteemed him not.

Surely, he has borne our griefs and carried our sorrows;

Yet we esteemed him stricken, smitten by God and afflicted.

But he was wounded for our transgressions, he was bruised for our iniquities;

Upon him was the chastisement that made us whole, and by his stripes we are healed.

All we like sheep have gone astray; we have turned every one to his own way;

And the Lord has laid upon him the iniquity of us all" (Is 53:4-6).

May the grace of the mystery of the Scourging at the Pillar come down into our hearts.

3

THE CROWNING WITH THORNS

"And the soldiers plaited a crown of thorns and put it on his head and arrayed him in a purple robe; they came up to him, saying, "Hail, King of the Jews!" and struck him with their hands. Pilate went out again, and said to them, "Behold, I am bringing him out to you, that you may know that I find no crime in him." So Jesus came out, wearing a crown of thorns and a purple robe. And Pilate said to them, "Behold the Man!" (Jn 19 1-5)

Behold the Man! Ecce Homo! Jesus, crowned with thorns, a reed-scepter thrust in his bound hands, clothed with the centurion's scarlet cloak glued to every bleeding wound is mockingly displayed to the mob demanding his death. Pilate, deriding both Jesus and the Jewish people, cries out: "What shall I do with your *King?*"

The eternal and incarnate Wisdom, our God in a fully human way, is put on display as the world's fool! The Creator is mocked by his creatures. Infinite Love is scorned by his own. The crowd shouts back the horrendous rejection of its Savior: "We have no King but Caesar!" "Then what shall I do with your *King?*", demands the Roman Procurator. And the mob responds in words which make the cosmos tremble: "Crucify him, Crucify him!" (Jn 19:6).

But listen attentively to the cries of the crowd. Can you hear your voice shouting with them, "Away with him — He is not our King?" A Roman Procurator, a motley element of Jewish leadership which is considered degraded by the people, are they the cause of Jesus' death? Scripture says, "He was wounded for *our* transgressions. He has borne *our* sins and carried *our* sorrows." The tiny group of the world's population which cried out for Jesus' death on that first Good Friday were representatives of the universe — each one of us — which bears responsibility for the death of the Lord.

How often have we not cried out: "We have no King but Caesar?" And "Caesar" is our own way, our own pleasure, even though it may entail the rejection of the radical demands of the gospel. How often have we vetoed the kingship of Christ by being afraid to proclaim the truth of our faith with bold clarity. How often have we found excuses for the betrayal of our faith — and therefore of Jesus — by appealing to the so-called custom of "compromise"? Whenever we water down our witness to the gospel by the way we live, by the way we speak, by the way we teach or preach, are we not shouting, "Away with him, we have no King but Caesar?" With Saint Paul, we must admit that we have crucified the Lord of glory!

The enormity of our sins, of our betrayal of our King, Jesus the Lord, is seen with such awesome clarity in the third sorrowful mystery, **The Crowning with Thorns**. Danger is that we constantly go back to the Praetorium of Pilate and with an unconscious self-righteousness, damn all those who rejected the King of kings and Lord of lords. The rosary is not meant to be an indictment against Pilate or the small band of renegade Jewish leaders! It rather confronts **us** with our own deep-seated sinfulness. With Mary, the Mother of the thorn-crowned King, we plead for mercy, pardon, forgiveness. And even more — we beg the strength to always remain faithful to the Lord of All, the King whom the "world" still mocks so ferociously by its "democratic permissiveness."

Would it be possible to turn our backs on our King if we daily meditated on the rosary? Would it be likely that anyone who with Mary contemplates the *Ecce Homo* would continue in sin? Hardly! To gaze daily on the mystery of the crowning with thorns strengthens us to live the Good News to the hilt, to refuse all compromise of our faith, no matter the jibes and mockery of the "world," to be faithful — no matter the cost — to Christ the King.

There are many inscriptions of the reigning Caesar crowned with a mighty diadem with spikes protruding from it to signify power, awe, majesty, if not even claimed divinity! When Jesus was thrown to the wishes of a battalion (five hundred) of soldiers, the beatings and incredible insults he endured are beyond our imagination. He — our eternal and incarnate God, enfleshed infinite Love — is made the butt of torture and diabolical blasphemies. It is, as John tells us, *the hour of satan,* the hour of darkness. Infinite incarnate Light must endure the depth of the darkness of human depravity in order to rescue us from its grip. Scripture stresses one of the worst: the mocking of Jesus *as if* he were a king. The thorns will imitate the spiked crown of Caesar, the reed, his scepter, the soldier's cloak, Caesar's royal garment. Carved into the stones of the soldiers' barracks are traces of games, like blind-man's bluff. Who better to be the target of these games than the one who is claimed to be "King" of the Jews? Saint Louis de Montfort sings a dirge concerning this mystery: Jesus' eyes being bound with a dirty rag, slapped, whipped, spit upon, abused. "Prophesy to us," the soldiers cry mockingly, "who is it who struck you!" He who reigns over all, the Lord of earth and sky, is so ironically mocked as king!

But the derision of Jesus as the king goes to even further extremes. Herod is in Jerusalem for the feast of the Passover. Pilate, perhaps thinking that he could get rid of all responsibility in this case, sends the beaten, tortured, thorn-crowned Jesus to Herod (cf Lk 23:7-12). After all, is not Herod in charge of Galilee? And is not Jesus a Galilean?

Herod welcomes the opportunity to see Jesus who has been acclaimed by so many of the simple people, especially the outcasts, the sinners. As Herod — who had murdered John the Baptizer — demands some sign from this "wonder-worker," Jesus remains totally silent. Herod in anger labels him a fool. "Like a lamb that is led to the slaughter, and like a sheep that before its shearers is dumb, so he opened not his mouth" (Is 53:7). In angry jest, Herod has Jesus' clothes torn from his bleeding body, and garbs his torn flesh with a resplendent cloak. *Eternal Wisdom* mocked as *The Fool!*

When Jesus is returned to Pilate, the Roman Procurator decides to rid himself completely of this man Jesus and hand him over to the crowds. The representative of Caesar, condemns the King of kings to death.

Etched forever in the conscience of humankind is the picture of the *Ecce Homo*. A condemnation of this "world?" Yes, but even more so, a sign of the infinite Love who is God. "For us and for our salvation," he is crowned with thorns, mocked, derided, so that we may rise out of our folly into the life of eternal Wisdom himself.

The third sorrowful mystery is intertwined with the truth that Christ is truly our King. He, the Lord of All, has conquered us by his suffering and death. Yet we must remember the insistence of Jesus that he is our servant. A King who is the slave of his subjects? Such is the mystery of infinite Love. Jesus is the King who serves. To claim the kingship of Jesus is to recognize that he is *for us*. The King awaits our loving command: "Ask and it will be given to you; seek and you will find; knock and it will be opened to you" (Lk 11:9). The King always responds to his people. In fact, he answers with that "excess of meaning" so characteristic of his person. Even more than we ask the King will give us if we ask with loving boldness, with firm faith. Although so often hidden from our eyes, the answer of Jesus goes beyond our hopes and expectations. In total surrender to the King of infinite Love for us, we "ask" knowing that we shall always "receive," not precisely what we may request but far more. Our thorn-crowned King yearns to serve us.

May the grace of the mystery of the Crowning with Thorns come down into our hearts.

4
THE CARRYING OF THE CROSS

Essential to evangelical spirituality is the mystery of the cross. It is not surprising then that we find it with such emphasis in the spirituality of Saint Louis de Montfort. Like a golden thread it is woven throughout his life, his preaching and his writings. Any attempt to discard it results in the unraveling of the tapestry itself of Montfort spirituality. Eleven hymns — and numerous stanzas of others — are devoted to *The Cross*. One of the saint's most powerful works is his contemplative yet so practical *Letter to the Friends of the Cross*, a meditation on "the remarkable words of our Savior," "If anyone wants to be a follower of mine, let him renounce himself, and take up his cross and follow me (Mt 16:24; Lk 9:23)." Moreover it should never be forgotten that Montfort's foundational composition, *The Love of the Eternal Wisdom*, contains a central section on *The Triumph of Eternal Wisdom in and by the Cross*. The conclusion of 180 of *The Love of the Eternal Wisdom* summarizes Montfort's mystical insight into the mystery of the cross: "Eternal Wisdom (Jesus Christ) has fixed his abode in the cross so firmly that you will not find him anywhere in this world except in the cross. He has so truly incorporated and united himself with the cross that in all truth we can say: *Wisdom is the cross and the cross is Wisdom*."

Boldly, Montfort speaks of the practical results of meditation on this fourth sorrowful mystery of the rosary: "Wise and honest people living in this world, you do not understand the mysterious language of the cross. You are too fond of sensual pleasures and you seek your comforts too much. You have too much regard for the things of this world and you are too afraid to be held up to scorn or looked down upon. In short, you are too opposed to the cross of Jesus. True, you speak well of the cross in general but not of the one that comes your way. You shun this as much as you can or else drag it along reluctantly, grumbling, impatient and protesting. I seem to see in you the oxen that drew the ark of the covenant against their will, bellowing as they went, unaware that what they were drawing contained the most precious treasure upon earth....But, true disciples of Eternal Wisdom, if you have trials and afflictions, if you suffer much persecution for justice' sake, if you are treated as the refuse of the world, be comforted, rejoice, be glad and dance for joy because the cross you carry is a gift so precious as to arouse the envy of the saints in heaven...." (*Love of the Eternal Wisdom*, 178-179).

For the Roman overlords, the cross was the most horrendous instrument of execution that could be devised. Only criminals who could make no claim to Roman citizenship would undergo such torture for it was synonymous with total degradation, failure, disgrace, incredible suffering, ignominious death. Cicero, in fact, tells us that the terms *cross, crucifixion*, are never to be spoken in polite society, so disgusting are they. The Old Testament itself proclaims: "Cursed be everyone who hangs upon a tree" (Gal 3:13 cf Dt 21:23); so horrible is the *tree of the cross* that anyone who hangs upon it must, so the Jews believed, be damned by God. The cross is, therefore, as Paul declares, a "stumbling block to the Jews and folly to the Gentiles but to those who are called, both Jews and Greeks, Christ the power of God and the wisdom of God" (1 Cor 1:23-25).

The cross becomes also the symbol of the folly, the sinfulness of the human race. Its weight is not measured by the timber but by the incalculable guilt of every sin of each member of the human family. "He has borne our griefs and carried our sorrows" (Is 53:4).

When Pilate "handed Jesus over to them to be crucified"

(Jn 19:16), an event of cosmic proportion begins to unfold. Infinite incarnate Holiness embraces the horrifying cross and takes on the damnation of us all. Not reluctantly but with infinite love.

The cross now becomes the instrument of the death of the Savior and thereby the means of victorious redemption for us. Eternal Wisdom takes on the folly of the cross so that our sinful folly may be transformed into Wisdom.

Jesus, beaten, crowned with thorns, falling under the weight of the cross of our rebellion, stumbles along the *via dolorosa*. Afraid that Jesus may die before reaching Golgotha, the Romans force a passer-by, Simon of Cyrene, to assist Jesus (cf Mk 15:21). Little does he understand that the cross he carries is the salvation of the world!

Luke also tells us of some faithful women wailing and consoling the blood-stained Jesus as he staggers, half-dead, on the narrow path to Calvary. Tradition identifies two of these women: Veronica, who offers a clean cloth to Jesus upon which his tortured portrait becomes indelibly imprinted, and Mary, his mother. The consolation the mother's bravery gives to the Son is great indeed; greater still, the suffering overwhelming her at the terrible sight of the Child she bore. The sword of dying with Christ pierces, as Simeon prophesied, ever more deeply into her immaculate heart.

Three times, tradition tells us, Jesus stumbles and falls under the weight of the cross. Three times he begins again the journey to Calvary, no matter the pain. Upon reaching Golgotha, the Place of the Skull, Jesus is stripped of his garments. As the soldiers tear away his clothes, every wound is reopened. Crowned with thorns, blood pouring forth from his wounds, the eternal and incarnate Wisdom is displayed naked before the mocking world.

Stripped of everything. Only those who surrender all can share the cross. Poverty is a keyword in the gospel proclamation. Anything or anyone who keeps us back from union with Jesus is considered *diabolical* (cf *True Devotion*, 62). Yet how tenaciously we grasp our idols, how fearful we are to let go of our treasures. Nations — and individuals — will even destroy each other in order to retain the golden calves of pride, prestige, wealth. Like the rich young man, we turn away from Jesus because of our many possessions. Simplicity of life, a characteristic of the christian who embraces the cross, must be the expression of an interior poverty. The wealth of *doing our own thing*, of demanding our own way, of *using* others, of trying to *possess others*, of seeking our own pleasures no matter how repulsive to the law of Christ: all must be stripped from us. Otherwise we cannot be crucified with Christ. If we are not crucified with the Lord, we shall not reign with the Lord. The first beatitude which summarizes them all, tells us that only the poor enter the kingdom of God.

Forcibly stripped, the King of glory is displayed naked before the scoffing world. Sensuality, *sex as toy*, the deification of the *body-beautiful*, the blatant, fashionable immodesty: all must be atoned by the Word made flesh. The strength of the sorrowful mysteries is found in its power to impress deep within us not only the love of God but also our rejection of that love by blasphemously making ourselves gods.

We cannot meditate on this fourth sorrowful mystery without concluding, *"Never the cross without Jesus, or Jesus without the cross"* (*Love of the Eternal Wisdom*, 172). The identification of Divine Wisdom and the cross means that the cross is essential to christianity. Does not Jesus teach this to us repeatedly? "If any man would come after me, let him deny himself and take up his cross daily and follow me...whoever does not bear his own cross and come after me, cannot be my disciple" (Lk 9:23; 15:21). The cross — our daily dyings with Christ — if borne with Jesus, implement the victory won by the triumphant cross of the Savior.

''The cross is precious,'' writes Montfort, ''because when it is well carried it is the source, the food and the proof of love. The cross enkindles the fire of divine love in the heart by detaching it from creatures. It keeps this love alive and intensifies it; as wood is the food of flames, so the cross is the food of love. And it is the soundest proof that we love God. The cross was the proof God gave of his love for us and it is also the proof which God requires to show our love for him'' (*Love of the Eternal Wisdom*, 176).

Montfort's life demonstrates this truth so powerfully. Expelled from one diocese after another because of his fidelity to the Holy Father and his unconditional living of the gospel, he saw these ''defeats'' as privileged crosses bringing him to the conquest of souls for Christ. Although he suffered unjustly — as he himself complains — he united these crosses with the cross of the Savior and turned them into victories. *What a cross to be without a cross*, became his often repeated remark. Father de Montfort was paraphrasing the inspired words of Scripture: ''For the word of the cross is folly to those who are perishing but to us who are being saved it is the power of God...far be it from me to glory except in the cross of our Lord Jesus Christ'' (1 Cor 1:18; Gal 6:14).

The cross is our emblem. The cross is our flag. The cross is our standard. It precedes us in every liturgical procession for it leads us on life's pilgrimage to our eternal home.

May the grace of the mystery of the Carrying of the Cross come down into our hearts.

5
THE CRUCIFIXION

" **H**e who hangs upon a tree is accursed of God" (Dt 21:23). In such severe terms, Scripture promulgates that whosoever is crucified has incurred the damnation of God. The fifth sorrowful mystery of the rosary fixes our contemplative gaze on Jesus crucified who takes on the condemnation of us all.

The horrors of that first Good Friday exceed the limits of human language. We can only approximate a description of that blackest day in the history of the universe. On the hill of Golgotha outside Jerusalem's walls, the soldiers rip off Jesus' robe, now glued to his torn body so drenched with blood. Every wound now bleeds profusely. Stretched out upon the wood of the cross, his hands are nailed to the crossbeam which is then attached to the upright beam already in place. His feet are now nailed to the cross, his ripped, naked body supported by a flat peg protruding from it. The beaten *Criminal* is elevated no more than a foot or two above the ground. Jesus, stripped, scourged, mocked, reviled, scorned, now hangs in public view for the last few hours of his agonizing dying. The universe itself shudders at the sight: "Now from the sixth hour there was darkness over all the land until the ninth hour...and behold, the curtain of the temple was torn in two, from top to bottom, the earth shook and the rocks were split..." (Mt 27:45, 51).

With Jesus Crucified is his mother Mary. "Even at his death she had to be present so that he might be united with her in one sacrifice and be immolated with her consent to the eternal Father, just as formerly Isaac was offered in sacrifice by Abraham when he accepted the will of God. It was Mary who nursed him, fed him, cared for him, reared him and sacrificed him for us" (*True Devotion*, 18). The woman of faith surrenders at the cross even more intensely than she did at the Annunciation. Her *Yes* in the name of the entire cosmos forms part of the full picture of Calvary. In the name of all yearning for redemption, she surrenders her Divine Son through her salvific *Yes* to the mysterious will of God.

From the cross, Jesus promulgates Mary's universal motherhood, her spiritual maternity; "Standing by the cross were his mother and his mother's sister, Mary the wife of Clopas, and Mary Magdalene. When Jesus saw his mother and the disciple whom he loved standing near, he said to his mother, 'Woman, behold your son!' Then he said to the disciple, 'Behold your mother!' And from that hour the disciple took her into his home" (Jn 19:25-27).

The faithful disciple, the symbol of all followers of Jesus, takes Mary "into his home." She is now his and he is her son. All christians are to be known as her children. She is the mother of all the followers of Christ; she is the mother of the church.

The little company of Mary, faithful, strong, stands bravely at the foot of the cross, proud to be identified with the "Lawbreaker" hanging upon the tree. After three hours of unspeakable torture, Jesus collapses in death, breathing a sign of love to his *Abba*: "Father, into thy hands, I commit my spirit" (Lk 23:46).

A crucifixion is a bloodcurdling sight. However, to reflect only on the torment inflicted upon Jesus is not a rosary meditation. Saint Louis de Montfort's writings call us to deeper contemplation, requesting that we meditate upon three questions: *Who is dying on the cross? Why is He dying? What are the repercussions of his death?*

Who is dying on the cross? Hundreds of criminals were crucified during the years when Pontius Pilate was procurator in Jerusalem. What is it that makes the execution of

Jesus so unique? It is not primarily the intensity of the torment wrought on Jesus; rather, it is the *Person* of Jesus which makes his death so horrible and at the same time, redemptive. This man Jesus is personally our God. He who hangs upon the tree is the eternal and incarnate Wisdom of the Father. He is our God in a fully human way. *We have crucified the Lord of Glory!* (cf. 1 Cor 2:8). Creation is executing its incarnate Creator. The Word made flesh is being slain by his own. The sin of the world has reached its climactic distortion.

Jesus is the Wisdom of God personally expressed in and through our folly; the Love of God personally manifested in and through our estrangement; the Power of God personally revealed in and through our weakness. Jesus, as the peak of creation's union with God, is its all-inclusive summary and representative. As the final, victorious Word of the Father, all creation derives its ultimate meaning from him. "All things were created in him and for him. He is before all things and in him all things hold together" (Col 1:16-17). The human race is executing its loving Brother, the incarnate Word of God "who for us and our salvation became man."

In one of the most beautiful pages of the *True Devotion*, Saint Louis de Montfort describes who Jesus crucified is: "In him alone dwells the entire fullness of the divinity and the complete fullness of grace, virtue and perfection...He is the only teacher from whom we must learn; the only Lord on whom we should depend; the only Head to whom we should be united and the only model we should imitate. He is the only Physician who can heal us, the only Shepherd who can feed us, the only Way that can lead us, the only Truth that we can believe, the only Life that can animate us. He alone is everything to us and he alone can satisfy all our desires. We are given no other name under heaven by which we can be saved. God has laid no other foundation for our salvation, perfection and glory than Jesus..." (*True Devotion*, 61). Yet, in spite of such beauty and grandeur, on Good Friday humankind murdered its incarnate God, Jesus the Lord.

Why is Jesus dying on the cross? The Romans would say, as the inscription on the cross advertised, that Jesus was being put to death because He was a ringleader of a rebellion against Caesar, that He pretended to be the *King of the Jews*. Some of the leaders of his people believed him to be a blasphemer for He called God his *Abba* and broke the sabbath (cf Jn 5:18). How far from the mark!

Jesus dies "for us and for our salvation." As the climactic point of creation's union with God, he is the summary of the entire cosmos: "In him all things hold together" (Col 1:17). He is the representative of us all, upon him are all our sins and our sorrows (cf Is 53). Jesus, although so caught up in the horrors of crucifixion, dies in loving harmony with the Father, out of love for us. His voice, his heart, are the voice and heart of this rebellious creation and in him, all creation now cries out in love to the Father. His arms outstretched in an eternal call of love, He dies as He lives: *for us*. The trumped up charges of his enemies cannot destroy the truth that the Wisdom of the Father has assumed all of sinful humanity — and therefore our death — out of love for us. For Jesus himself has stated that he has come to serve us, that he is for us (cf Mk 10:45).

Since Jesus' entire being is *for us*, so too his death is *for us*. Death is not just a rupture from without; it is a fulfillment from within. Jesus, therefore, dies as he lives: *for others*. His death is the full realization of his *being-for-us*.

What are the repercussions of Jesus' death? Saint Louis de Montfort joins in with the early Fathers of the church in calling the cross the *Tree of Life*. In the Garden of Eden, humankind enters into rebellion against God through a tree, a man and a woman: the tree of the knowledge of good

and evil; a man, Adam; a woman, Eve. In their disobedience they ate the fruit of the tree thereby forever closing
off entry to the **Tree of Life**. Scripture closes the account of
the first sin with the tragic words: "And the Lord God drove
out the man; and at the east of the garden of Eden he placed
the cherubim and a flaming sword which turned every
way, to guard the way to the tree of life" (Gen 3:24). Access
to Life is closed because of the rebellion which now marks
the human race.

In Calvary's garden, we have the reversal of the calamity
of the Garden of Eden. Humankind is restored to harmony
with God through a tree, a man and a woman: the tree of
life, the cross; the New Adam, Jesus, and the New Eve,
Mary. On the tree of Golgotha hangs the fruit which alone
can give eternal life, Jesus, the food of Life come down from
heaven (cf Jn 6). Access is now open to the tree of life.
Whosoever goes to the tree, plucks its eucharistic fruit and
eats of it, has life eternal and will be raised up on the last
day. Through the water flowing from his pierced side we
are reborn. The blood poured out is our eucharistic drink.
The tree of life has been restored to the human family.
"Then he showed me the river of the water of life, bright as
crystal flowing from the throne of God and of the
Lamb...also, on either side of the river, the Tree of
Life...and the leaves of the tree were for the healing of the
nations" (Rev 22:1-2). Victory over sin and eternal death is
won in the same way that life was lost, through a tree, a
man and a woman.

What, then are the repercussions of the once-and-for-all
sacrifice of Christ upon the cross? Estrangement is conquered by infinite Love, sin by infinite Obedience,
darkness by eternal Light, death by divine Life, folly by the
eternal and incarnate Wisdom. The cross is our *victorious*
standard, our glorious banner, drawing us to the food of

eternal life which hangs upon it, Jesus the Lord. *Behold the wood of the cross*, sings the church on Good Friday, *on which hung our salvation.*

> *May the grace of the mystery of the Crucifixion come down into our hearts.*

The Glorious Mysteries

INTRODUCTION

The rosary, like the gospels, concludes on the jubilant note of victory! The glorious mysteries not only recall the resplendent conquest of Jesus over our sin and death but even more so, actually insert us into his triumph. By the contemplation of the victorious mysteries of the rosary, we too become conquerors, we share ever more intensely in the glory of Christ-Victor. Since the rosary is so profoundly an integration of the gospels in our lives, its daily recitation strengthens us, forms us, re-creates us into the image of Jesus, the victorious Risen Lord.

In the final episode of the sorrowful mysteries, we stood with Mary on Calvary and contemplated the eternal and in-carnate Wisdom executed on the gibbet of the cross. Creation had plunged to its nadir; the sin of the world had reached its culmination, for we crucified the Lord.

However, if the history of Jesus ended on Calvary, if the crucifixion were the final mystery, then we would of all people be the most foolish (cf 1 Cor 15:19). Jesus would be *The Great Failure*. The story of Jesus would be no more than a textbook footnote. The world would still be in sin. The final word spoken over this cosmos would be *Death.*

But that is not the reality! "The Lord has risen indeed and has appeared to Simon!" (Lk 24:34). And we boldly pro-claim with Paul: "Death is swallowed up in victory...Thanks be to God who has given us the victory through our Lord Jesus Christ" (1 Cor 15:54, 57). Jesus is victorious over death. The final and eternal chapter of salvation history is *victory!* The destiny of this universe is to share in the glory of God.

Through the faith-filled contemplation of the glorious mysteries, we renew our baptism into *new* Life, we recall that we are citizens of the victorious *new* creation. The rebellion has been quelled. A harmony now prevails among ourselves, with ourselves, for in Jesus triumphant we are once again in harmony with the ground of all being, God. True, the victory is not fully implemented! However, the glorious mysteries draw us ever more deeply into this *new* victorious life.

New Life? Why *new* life? Would it not be sufficient if the conquest through the cross/resurrection just made this world a better place to live where there would be no sickness or death and all would be peaceful? By no means. To be doomed to this existence forever is not the will of God; it is not the yearning of the human heart. Without any goal, with endless tomorrows never reaching fulfillment, would be the hell of empty meaninglessness. No matter how magnificent the train, it becomes torment if we are doomed to remain on it forever with no aim, no final destination. But such is not the plan of God. We are created with a goal, a clear destination: to share in the power of the Spirit, through the victorious Christ, in eternal, infinite Love who is God.

The human heart is never fulfilled by natural beauty, no matter how resplendent. The destiny God has implanted into the fiber of our being is himself, infinite, eternal Love. No human love — of its nature finite, limited — no matter how thrilling, no matter how faithful, can be the consummation of a heart endowed with the capacity for the Infinite. Only in God can the human being find rest and full realization.

On the other hand, such a goal is not within the power of finite human beings. The Tower of Babel has long since shown that there is no possibility of building a "stairway to the stars." In spite of some utopian claims, no advances can ever transform this universe into that perfect, infinite harmony for which the heart was made. Often so called progress heightens frustration, like the earth-shattering bombs, the impersonalism of modern medical technology. No, God has not made us for a *better* world. Our goal is eternal life in the *new* creation of infinite Love, to be children of the New Adam, the glorious, triumphant Jesus.

It is Jesus who through his victorious death/resurrection, has opened up the prison of this finite cosmos to the freedom of the infinite glory of God. He alone is the Way. He alone is Life. He is the opening to glory. Auto- or self-redemption is clearly impossible for creatures. It is Jesus, the God-Man, who frees us. In him, glory is our goal, infinite Love our destination, eternal *new* life our destiny.

Such is the magnificent theme of the glorious mysteries of the rosary. Beginning with the resurrection of Jesus, they unfold to the vision of the parousia when with Mary, the faithful disciple, we shall reign in glory forever and ever. The glorious mysteries of the rosary are the final, jubilant melody of the symphony of history.

1

THE RESURRECTION

One of the earliest proclamations of the resurrection of Jesus is probably the short catechism lesson which Paul inserts in his *First Letter to the Corinthians*:

"For I delivered to you as of first importance what I also received: that Christ died for our sins in accordance with the scriptures, that he was buried, that he was raised on the third day in accordance with the scriptures, and that he appeared to Cephas, then to the twelve. Then he appeared to more than five hundred brethren at one time, most of whom are still alive, though some have fallen asleep. Then he appeared to James, then to all the apostles" (15:3-7).

Paul learned this formula shortly after his conversion on the road to Damascus. It summarizes the content of the first glorious mystery of the rosary.

The central teaching of the early christians is that Jesus, truly dead, truly buried, rose victorious on the third day and made himself to be seen by chosen witnesses. Can it therefore be said that three days after his death, Jesus returned to *this* life?

Although so central to christianity, the Easter event is misunderstood by many followers of Christ. For too many it means that Jesus returned to *this* life after his burial, spent forty days with his disciples and then rocket-like ascended to the Father.

Our time-bound situation makes it difficult to express an event which is beyond time and space categories. Jesus is the *New Adam*, inaugurating a *new creation*. The resurrection is definitely *not* a *Lazarus-event*. The brother of Martha and Mary was raised by Jesus; however, Lazarus returned to *this* life with all its limitations and weaknesses and one day suffered illness and finally, death. But the risen Jesus dies no more; in the fullness of his being, he is in the realm of his ABBA, the Father. Locked doors and closed windows, then, offer no resistance to his unexpected appearances, for he is *radically* transformed, eternally transfigured, suffused with the Spirit:

"So it is with the resurrection of the dead. What is sown is perishable, what is raised is imperishable. It is sown in dishonor, it is raised in glory...it is sown a physical body, it is raised a spiritual body" (l Cor 15:42-44).

Jesus Risen is the *first-born* of this *new* creation, He is the ultimate, final victory over sin and death. The identical Jesus who died upon the cross, the identical Jesus buried in the tomb is, victorious, transformed, transfigured, triumphant forevermore with Yahweh. It is from the realm of the glory of Yahweh that Jesus makes himself to be truly seen by chosen witnesses. Jesus does not walk out of the tomb and back into this world as Lazarus did. The power of his ABBA assumes his incarnate Beloved into infinite glory.

The sepulcher is empty. No matter what contemporary philosophy may conjecture about the necessity of a truly *bodily* resurrection, the word of God as constantly proclaimed by the church makes it clear that the body lying in the tomb has become the instrument of Christ's everlasting glory. "He is risen, he is not here, see the place where they laid him" (Mk 16:6). An element of this finite creation, the humanity of Jesus, is now exalted, glorious with the Father. Jesus does not discard his humanity at the resurrection for the eternal Word of God is forever *enfleshed*. He remains forever one of us, the Brother of us all, a part of this creation, interrelated with this world more than was ever possible when bound by the strict limitations of *this* life. In Christ Risen, therefore, we see the goal of all creation, of every molecule of matter, drawn by him to its ultimate fulfillment: Glory.

A *new age* has begun, a *new world* where suffering, crying and death are no more. "Behold, I make all things new," (Rev 21:5) says the risen Lord.

Jesus risen is the *victorious Lord* over all, the *New Adam of the new creation*, the *Conqueror of sin and death*. To deny the Resurrection of Jesus is to deny christianity itself. The New Testament is founded upon this fundamental proclamation: *Jesus is risen!* Without that belief there would be no possibility of stating that "the Word became flesh" (Jn 1:14), no reason whatsoever for a community of believers.

Does not Jesus summarize all creation? As the personal *externalization* of the eternal Beloved of the Father, Jesus encapsulates the entire cosmos. Everything Jesus says and does is *for us, in our name*. He dies *for us*. He is risen *for us*, "for our justification" (Rom 4:25). As Paul so often states, we die *with* Christ, we rise *with* Christ. Then in Christ, *we* are victorious! Battles may be lost, but the war has been won in Christ Jesus risen! We do not know the intervening chapters of history, but the final, decisive chapter has already been published: *victory!* Humankind's purpose does not come from *within* history; its certain, victorious goal is the risen Lord. As in a play, the climactic scene renders everything before and after it intelligible, so too in history, its climactic moment — the resurrection of the eternal and incarnate Wisdom — is the fundamental insight into the meaning of this universe and its history. The goal of the cosmos is anticipated in the Easter event; to be one with the Risen Christ in the power of the Holy Spirit, so that through the victorious Lord we may be one with God the Father for all eternity.

As we meditate upon the first glorious mystery, we are filled with hope. Not that the world is always on an *upward* evolutionary spiral. Present events, with the possibility of atomic holocausts contradict such interpretation. Yet, the *final* outcome — without knowing precisely how it will be achieved — is joyfully proclaimed by Paul: the victory is ours through our Lord Jesus Christ (cf 1 Cor 15:57). Everything we say, everything we do, everything we suffer must always be seen *only* against the backdrop of the *victorious* cross. Vibrant faith in the resurrection brings about a joyful transformation of our attitudes and outlook. Even the worst calamity cannot destroy our belief that we are eternally, unconditionally, victoriously loved. All crosses become lightened for we know that Calvary leads to the empty tomb. Faith leads not to death but to eternal victorious life: the risen Christ Jesus, our Lord!

Saint Louis de Montfort's *Night Prayers* call upon his religious congregations, the Daughters of Wisdom and the Montfort Missionaries, to end the day with this beautiful prayer: "My Savior, Jesus Christ, we offer you our sleep in honor of and in union with your sleep, your death and your burial; and our awakening tomorrow in honor of and in union with your holy resurrection. We adore your holy sentiments in these actions and we beg of you the grace to make them our own." Saint Louis de Montfort would want our first thoughts on awakening to be that Jesus is risen, that the cross is *victorious. We are people of hope! We are people of joy!* Everything during the day is seen against the victorious horizon of the first glorious mystery of the rosary, the Resurrection.

> *May the grace of the mystery of the resurrection*
> *come down into our hearts.*

2

THE ASCENSION

The second glorious mystery, the Ascension, is a contemplation of the summit of our redemption: having completed his work of salvation, the Redeemer returns triumphant into the glory of the Father.

In order to grasp the full meaning of this decade of the rosary, there is a fundamental question we have to answer. Who is the *Beloved* of God?

Since God is Love Itself, there must be a *Beloved*, otherwise how could we declare that God IS dynamic Love? (cf 1 Jn 4:8, 16). *Lover* always presupposes a *Beloved*. Who is the *Beloved* of God?

No, don't rush to say: *We are!* Stop for a moment. Whoever this *Beloved* is, the person exists from all eternity since from the beginning God is Love. Moreover, this *Beloved* is intrinsic to the very being of God — there cannot be *Lover* without a *Beloved*. Therefore neither creation as a whole nor human beings can be THE Beloved. We are not from all eternity; we are in no way intrinsic to the very being of God. Rather, we are God's free gift, not at all *necessary* to God. Who then can be God's *Beloved*?

The Beloved can only be found within God himself. Since it cannot be creation, or anything outside of God — all exists as pure gift — the Beloved is *within* the very being of God. God is Lover who pours himself out within the divine Life and in so doing, is the source of the co-equal Beloved. Saint Louis de Montfort speaks of the Beloved as the *eternal Wisdom of the Father*. The Son, the eternal Word, is, says Montfort, the very goodness of the Father, the infinite eternal brightness of God. Wisdom "is a breath of the power of God, a pure emanation of the glory of the Almighty...a reflection of eternal light, a spotless mirror of the working of God, and an image of his goodness'' (Wisdom, 7:25, ff. cf. *Love of the Eternal Wisdom*, 16-18).

It is the will of the Father from all eternity to express his infinite Beloved *outside* of the divine Life, for us. Therefore, God wills a creation, a world, human beings whose very reason for being is to hear this one Word of the Father's vocabulary, to be penetrated with the life of the Beloved and to become *beloved in the Beloved* (cf Eph 13-10). Even when humankind rebels — from the first moment of its existence — God still wills to exteriorize his Beloved.

The Beloved, Wisdom incarnate, is, therefore, born into this sinful, rebellious world through the faith of Mary. The Beloved of the Father is conceived and borne in her womb and from her he comes forth on Christmas night. He, the infinite Beloved, is always and forever, the Son of Mary. He is sent into this rebellious family to restore us to God's friendship. For us he lives, for us he dies, for us he rises victorious.

The mystery of the Ascension is the celebration of the victorious exaltation of the incarnate Beloved, the "return" of the *Enfleshed Beloved* to the Lover. As Beloved, He has never left the Lover; but as *incarnate* Beloved He has "emptied himself, taking on the form of a slave" (Phil 2:6), manifested himself personally in and through our limitations, our finite rebellious humanity. Now victorious through the cross and resurrection, he is exalted — in his humanity! — and in this transformed humanity enters the realm of the Lover, the Father.

As the Incarnation is the entry of the Beloved into our human family, the Ascension is the return of the *incarnate* Beloved — forever a member of the human family — into the Lover. The ascension then completes the victory and earthly career of Jesus, the enfleshed Beloved, and marks the climax of the process of salvation. "I glorified thee on earth, having accomplished the work which thou gavest me to do; and now, Father, glorify thou me in thy own presence with the glory which I had with thee before the world was made" (Jn 17:4).

Having manifested himself in his glorious, triumphant, risen Body to chosen witnesses over a period of time, the Ascension marks the final Easter appearance of Jesus.

"As they were looking on, he was lifted up, and a cloud took him out of their sight. And while they were gazing into heaven as he went, behold, two men stood by them in white robes, and said, "Men of Galilee, why do you stand looking into heaven? This Jesus who was taken up from you into heaven, will come in the same way as you saw him go into heaven" (AA 1:9-11).

The next time we shall see the risen Lord — the incarnate, victorious Beloved — is at the *parousia*, the second coming.

The Ascension is then the celebration of the victorious incarnation, life, death and resurrection of Jesus. It is a compendium of the victorious incarnate Beloved who now is the triumphant Lord of the Universe.

There is another aspect of the second glorious mystery which cannot be overlooked. The Ascension is also the mandate to each one of us to implement this victory of the Beloved:

"Go therefore and make disciples of all nations, baptizing them in the name of the Father and of the Son and of the Holy Spirit, teaching them to observe all that I have commanded you..." (Mt 28: 19-20).

A characteristic of the appearance narratives is a commission to deliver the message of salvation. Intrinsic to the Easter appearances is the mandate that those who "see the Lord" are not only witnesses of the risen Christ but are also proclaimers of the good news of redemption. As narrated in the *Acts of the Apostles*, Jesus declares at the Ascension: "You shall receive power when the Holy Spirit comes upon you; and you shall be my witnesses in Jerusalem and in all Judea and Samaria and to the ends of the earth" (AA 1:8).

The sacraments are encounters with the risen Jesus. All christians, therefore, are commanded to evangelize, for all have "seen" the Lord especially through baptism and the eucharist. Intrinsic to the mystery of Christ's return to the Father, is the mandate that we be Christ in the world. Through us, the risen Lord reaches out to the poor, the lonely, the homeless. Through us, Christ continues to proclaim good news of salvation. As living gospels, we are to draw all people to the joy of the new creation, Jesus risen. What a transformation would occur in this world if all christians truly accepted this great mandate! By meditating on this second glorious mystery, the conviction of our privilege to be *heralds of glad tidings to the poor* becomes ever so clear.

May the grace of the mystery of the Ascension
come down into our hearts.

3

THE DESCENT OF THE HOLY SPIRIT

"They went up to the upper room, where they were staying...all these with one accord devoted themselves to prayer, together with the women and Mary the mother of Jesus, and with his brethren... When the day of Pentecost had come, they were all together in one place. And suddenly a sound came from heaven like the rush of a mighty wind and it filled all the house where they were sitting. And there appeared to them tongues as of fire, distributed and resting on each one of them. And they were all filled with the Holy Spirit and began to speak in other tongues as the Spirit gave them utterance" (AA 1:13-14; 2:1-4).

The third glorious mystery of the rosary, Pentecost, is both magnificent and difficult. Why? The primary party in the scene, the Holy Spirit, the Third Person of the Most Blessed Trinity, has been neglected in western thought. The early church experienced the problem, for we read in the *Acts of the Apostles*, that "Paul passed through the upper country and came to Ephesus. There he found some disciples. And he said to them, 'Did you receive the Holy Spirit when you believed?' And they said, 'No, we have never even heard that there is a Holy Spirit' " (19:1-2). Perhaps we can console ourselves by boasting that contemporary christians have surely heard that there is a Holy Spirit. But do we know who the Holy Spirit is? Many would say that the Spirit is the forgotten person of the Trinity. Who is this Spirit who comes with such transforming power upon the terrified disciples?

The meditation on the Ascension pointed out that the fundamental principle of all specifically christian reflection is that God is *triune*: one God, Father, Son and Holy Spirit. Since God *is* Love in person, then there must be a *Thou* of God: the

Beloved who becomes incarnate, Jesus the Lord. The Lover (*the Father*) and the Beloved (*the Son*) are bound together by infinite Loving: the *Holy Spirit*.

God discloses himself as triune Love, the three dynamic, interpenetrating relationships of Love: Lover, Beloved, Loving. The *Spirit* is pure *ecstasy* of the *Lover* and *Beloved*, pure *receiving* from the *Lover* through the *Beloved*, infinitely conjoining them.

Whenever we dare speak about our triune God, human language conceals more than it reveals. Or as stated clearly by the church, *God is more unlike anything we say about him than he is like it*. When we say that God is love, we have *concealed* God under our finite, limited understanding of the term *love*. For God is infinitely beyond our notion of *love*, so infinitely love that it is absolutely impossible for the human intellect to grasp the reality of the mystery who is God. Therefore, when it is stated that the Holy Spirit is the *infinite Loving* within the Godhead, the *Loving* of the *Lover* and the *Beloved*, the puny human mind is grappling with a *blinding* truth. That is why, often, when praying the third glorious mystery, we form no mental image of the first Pentecost. Rather, in a contemplative gaze, we release ourselves into the infinite *Loving* of God. And in the Spirit we are made one with the Father and the Son.

Pentecost is then the magnificent mystery of the sending of the *infinite Ecstasy* or *Loving* of the Godhead into our hearts. It is the *Lover* who through the *Beloved* sends forth the Spirit. John teaches this clearly: "... the Holy Spirit whom the Father will send in my name..." (Jn 14:26). At the Annunciation, the *Lover* sends the *Beloved* into our human family: Jesus, the incarnate Wisdom of God. At Pentecost, the *Lover*, through the *Beloved*, sends us their mutual *Loving*, thereby making us temples of the Holy Spirit. We are, in this sense, *divinized*, "partakers of the divine nature" (2 Pet 1:4).

Pentecost is not just a past event. Even in the *Acts of the Apostles,* we read not only of the pentecost at Jerusalem but also of other pentecosts, at Caesarea (cf 9:44-46) and at Ephesus (cf 19:6). At every moment, the infinite Loving is being sent into the core of our being. We can, therefore, call every second a pentecost, although the term is usually reserved for peak outpourings of the Spirit. How often, meditation on this third joyful mystery is truly a pentecost.

How can we be more open to the Holy Spirit? St. Louis de Montfort tells us: "The more the Spirit finds Mary, his dear and inseparable spouse in a soul, the more powerful and effective he becomes in producing Jesus Christ in that soul and that soul in Jesus Christ" (*True Devotion,* 20). If we lack the boldness of the early church, if our faith is so weak, then for Saint Louis de Montfort, the reason is evident. We are not men and women permeated with the Spirit of the Father and the Son for we are ignoring Mary, the woman of our race through whom the overshadowing Spirit forms the eternal and incarnate Wisdom. "One of the main reasons why the Holy Spirit does not now work striking wonders in souls is that he fails to find in them a sufficiently close union with his faithful and inseparable spouse, Mary" (*True Devotion,* 36; cf 20, 56-59, 214, *Prayer for Missionaries,* 15, 17). "Holy Spirit," prays Saint Louis de Montfort, "be ever mindful that it is you who, with Mary as your faithful Spouse, are to bring forth and fashion the children of God...All the saints who have ever existed or will exist until the end of time, will be the outcome of your love working through Mary" (*Prayer for Missionaries,* 15).

How much the contemporary world needs this *fiery deluge of pure love* as Montfort depicts the Spirit (cf *Prayer for Missionaries,* 17)! As we know from the first Pentecost, the Spirit impels us to leave the security of our own "upper room" and proclaim the word of redemptive Love with *boldness.* It is the Spirit who binds us together in love, who forms us into a truly loving, sharing community. The Spirit is, then, the source of love, peace, joy, which are the principal fruits of the Holy Spirit (cf Gal 5:22-23). Through the faith-filled meditation on the outpouring of the Holy Spirit, we too experience the presence of the infinite *Loving* of God. The wonders the infinite Spirit produces in us and through us by the rosary contemplation of Pentecost are beyond telling. No wonder that the third joyful mystery is of special importance to Saint Louis de Montfort. For his purpose is clear: to form an army of men and women, permeated with the infinite Spirit, which will "renew the face of the earth and reform the church" (cf *Prayer for Missionaries*, 17).

"Come, O Holy Spirit, Father of Lights, Come, O God of Charity!
Form in us a true spirit of prayer, Show us the Truth.
Pour into our hearts a burning coal of your Infinite Fire
To penetrate and fill us with Yourself, O Infinite Flame of God!"
(cf Saint Louis de Montfort, *Cantiques*, 141:1).

May the grace of the mystery of Pentecost
come down into our hearts.

4
THE ASSUMPTION

In 1950, His Holiness, Pope Pius XII, solemnly proclaimed a truth which has always existed in the church but which world circumstances now dictated be stated explicitly, dogmatically:

Mary, the Immaculate Mother of God, always a Virgin, after having completed the course of her earthly life, was taken body and soul into heavenly glory.

No one can doubt that Mary, the Spouse of the Holy Spirit, the virginal womb of God the Son, the beloved daughter of God the Father, now dwells forever in the glory of the Risen Lord. She who through faith carried in her womb the eternal and incarnate Wisdom, who is the immaculate Ark of the Covenant bearing the enfleshed Word of God, did not see the corruption of the tomb.

Jeremiah declares that the *Ark of the Old Testament*, made of incorruptible wood, would never be rebuilt after the destruction of the Temple by the Babylonians (Jer 3:16). The *New Testament Ark* is not a wooden box containing the two tablets of stone — for it will never be seen again — but a person, Mary, bearing the New Law, Jesus. The author of the *Book of Revelation* sees "the heavens opened and the Ark of his Covenant within his temple" (Rev 11:19). He then immediately describes the great sign in the heavens: "A woman clothed with the sun and on her head a crown of twelve stars" (Rev 12:1). The woman of *Revelation 12* is the symbol of the people of God; it is also Mary immaculate, the New Testament Ark, the pre-eminent member of the church and mother of God's people. In the fullness of her personality, she is assumed into the glory of her Divine Son, the temple of God.

Why *solemnly* and *dogmatically* promulgate this mystery? To extol the beauty of the faithful disciple, Mary the mother of God? Yes, but that is not the *ultimate* reason.

Consider the situation of the world shortly after World War II. Nations were trying to regain some equilibrium after years of devastation. However, the iron curtain had fallen along eastern Europe, the cold war had begun, the fear of atomic warfare had become a grim reality. The horrors of the *holocaust* were still vivid. Displaced persons were still searching for homes. Some countries, like the Baltic republics, had been wiped off the map. A pessimism promoted by atheistic existentialism filtered into the lives of many, especially through the publications of Sartre and Camus who wrote persuasively of human existence as absurd, meaningless.

The problem was not only political, sociological, philosophical. It was deeply religious. There was serious skepticism, if not outright denial, concerning the ultimate outcome of all creation, *eternal victory in Jesus Christ the risen Lord.*

The church, prompted by the Holy Spirit, responded with the solemn proclamation of the dogma of the Assumption. The model of the church, Mary, the summary of the universe both in its yearning for redemption and in its being divinized by Christ, shares gloriously in the fullness of her personality, in the eternal triumph of the risen Lord.

In her, we see *our victorious* goal. We have, therefore, not been made for nothingness, we are not destined to absurdity, we are not entrapped in meaninglessness. In the light of the Assumption of our sister, Mary, we see our goal in greater clarity: *one for all eternity with Christ Victor!*

An infallible statement of the church, the pillar and bulwark of truth (1 Tim 3:15), is a clear signpost pointing out the correct path. After the Second World War, it appeared that humankind was at a crossroad: meaninglessness or eternal life. The church intervened with the infallible evangelical cry: "Thanks be to God who has given *us* the victory through our Lord Jesus Christ" (1 Cor 15:57).

In response to the grave world situation, the church could have solemnly repeated the majestic chapter fifteen of *First Corinthians*. Paul insists upon our destiny which involves our entire being. However, following a custom of the church dating back to the times of the gospel, the church illuminates our situation by clarifying that of the first disciple of Jesus, the model of the church, Mary.

When examining the joyful mysteries, it became clear that Luke clarifies the meaning of faith by describing the woman of faith, Mary. In 1950, the church followed this evangelical example. Inspired by the Holy Spirit to proclaim infallibly that our goal is not destruction but joyful victory, the church does so through a description of Mary. As her faithful discipleship brought her, body and soul, into the eternal triumph of the risen Lord, so too our gospel fidelity will lead us not to emptiness but to the fullness of victory with Christ. Mary, in the glory of her Assumption is the shining lesson for all times that our destiny is heaven, the victorious risen Christ.

As we meditate, therefore, on this fourth glorious mystery of the rosary, we should not limit our thoughts to the glory of Mary's Assumption. For *whenever we talk about Mary we are ultimately talking about ourselves*, graced and redeemed by Christ. The Assumption stresses the victorious redemption gained **for us** by the death/resurrection of Jesus. Like everything authentically marian, it *magnifies the Lord*. As we contemplate Mary's Assumption, we should see *ourselves destined for glory*. The beautiful text "O death where is thy victory, O death where is thy sting?" (1 Cor 15:55) comes alive in the person of Mary assumed into heaven, reminding us that death is the passageway to eternal life.

Clearly, the mystery of Mary's Assumption has profound meaning for us today. Especially when we are tempted to pessimism and despair, when all seems so bleak and meaningless, the fourth glorious mystery illumines the day. Anxiety is felt strongly within the contemporary church at times without any specific object, at other times centered on the questions raised by radical feminism, ethics, fundamentalist cults, by the lack of vocations to the priestly and religious life. These are realities and it would be dangerous to ignore them. But nothing can be gained from fear. Discouragement, hopelessness, assure defeat. We must raise our eyes to the glory of the first disciple, Mary. She is the sign of sure hope that the victory of the risen Lord is the destiny of the cosmos. True, the *how* and the *when* are hidden from us. However, the Assumption teaches us that christians are to face the challenges of the age against the horizon of our sure *victory* with Christ, personified in Mary's Assumption.

A respect for the human body and for our extended body, the universe, is demanded by the truth of Mary's Assumption, for our entire person, body and soul, is called to glory. To abuse or deify the body is to ignore the reality of the Assumption.

The fourth joyful mystery is, therefore, one of profound hope for it opens our eyes to our ultimate glory. It is a rosary meditation which strengthens us to persevere in the struggle for justice for all peoples. It is the glorious mystery which continually challenges us to implement the triumph won for us by Christ Jesus.

Old age, death, so-called failures, loneliness, anxieties about the future, even our own sinfulness take on new meaning as we contemplate our destiny: like Mary the Ark, we shall be forever with the Lord. We should comfort one another with this truth (cf 1 Thes 4:18).

Mary is the first and the uniquely beloved. But *in her* all peoples and primarily the church whose form and model she is, are loved also. Her victory in Christ is an anticipation of the final goal of the church, of all the faithful disciples of Christ. The entire church, as Saint Ephraem writes, "rejoices in the Blessed Virgin Mary." And the entire church participates in her destiny: eternally glorious in the Holy Spirit, through Christ the Lord for the glory of God the Father.

May the grace of the mystery of the Assumption
come down into our hearts.

5
THE CORONATION
OF THE BLESSED VIRGIN MARY

Like the majestic, jubilant final *Amen* of Handel's *Messiah*, the rosary closes with the triumphant heavenly coronation of the Virgin Mary. Each note of the rosary has been a preparation for this royal trumpet-blast, the crowning of our Lady by our triune God. The first meditation, the Annunciation, announced the coming of the Messiah to save us; this final mystery proclaims the eternal victory of God's plan. We see Mary as "the woman crowned with twelve stars," (Rev 12:1) the infallible sign that all the followers of the victorious Lamb "will reign for ever and ever!" (Rev 22:5).

Like all the mysteries of the rosary, the Coronation of our Lady as Queen of Heaven centers on Jesus. It is only because of her pre-eminent sharing in the victorious grace of Christ the King that the triune God now crowns the faithful Mary. She is Queen *only* because her Son is King. Her queenship is a participation in the royalty of Christ. The kingship of Jesus is then the essential context of this final decade of the rosary.

Why is Jesus our King? First, He is the incarnate and eternal Wisdom of the Father, the personal expression of the *Beloved* in and through our humanity. He is the peak of all creation, our Brother who is our God enfleshed. He is, then, not someone who *becomes* King but He is the Lord of all from the first moment of his incarnation in Mary's womb. Christ is the King of this cosmos for he is not only to be honored, revered. He alone of all humanity is to be *adored*. He is mighty God incarnate.

Jesus has another title to kingship: he has conquered sin

and death through his death/resurrection. He has, as the sorrowful mysteries proclaim, vanquished us through love. He now wears the diadem for he wore the crown of thorns, for us. "I myself conquered," says Jesus-Amen of *Revelation,* "and sat down with my Father on his throne" (Rev 3:21). "Worthy is the Lamb who was slain, to receive power and wealth and wisdom and might and honor and glory and blessing!" (Rev 4:12). As Victor of the cosmos, He is "Lord of lords and King of kings" (Rev 17:14).

Why is Jesus King? All the reasons find their foundation in the bold statement: *He himself is the kingdom of God in Person.* He is the reign of Yahweh, infinite love poured out upon this broken creation. He calls each one of us to share in his life, to enter therefore into the kingdom and to reign with him: "He who conquers, I will grant him to sit with me on my throne" (Rev 3:21). In Christ Jesus, we are "a *royal* priesthood, a holy nation, God's own people" (1 Pet 2:9).

No one shares so intensely in the kingdom of God, the victorious risen Lord, than his immaculate Mother, Mary. No one reigns with him so uniquely as Mary, the maiden of Nazareth. For she is the mother of the King. Like the Queen-Mother of the kingdom of Judah, she sits upon a throne at the right of the monarch (cf 1 Kgs 2:19). The biblical theme of the queen-mother is brought to its fulfillment in Mary, Mother of the Messiah-King (cf Is 7:14; *True Devotion,* 76). Whoever accepts Jesus as King, will enthrone the queen-mother beside him.

Moreover, it is through her divinely-willed consent that the Word of God enters creation and as her divine Child, is the King of all his brothers and sisters. By her faith-participation in all the events of his life, including his death, she shares in a unique way in the royalty of her divine Son. She is inextricably united to her Son in his conquest; she then in a unique way shares in his royal glory: "Jesus, in choosing her as his inseparable associate in his life, death, glory and power in heaven and on earth, has given her *by grace* in his kingdom all the same rights and privileges that he possesses by nature" (*True Devotion*, 74).

Mary is also Queen because she is "full of grace" (Lk 1:28). Her sharing in the life of God is of such intensity that she rightly is called Queen of the Angels for she surpasses all creatures in her union with the Father, Son and Holy Spirit.

Pope Pius XII sums up this teaching in his encyclical, *Ad Coeli Reginam*: "Jesus Christ alone, God and Man, is King in the strict, full and absolute sense. Mary shares in his royal dignity in a secondary way, dependent on the sovereignty of her Son. She is the Mother of the Christ God and is his associate in the work of redemption, in his conflict with the enemy, and in his complete victory. It is from this union with Christ the King that she reaches a height of splendor unequaled in all creation."

Especially when meditating on this final decade of the rosary, it is important to "correct" some of the images of Mary-Queen, masterpieces though they may be. Often, art work depicts Mary as an ornate, distant, royal Empress. How far from the mark! After Jesus the King, there is no one more simple, more approachable, more loving than Mary the Queen. Mary's queenship is the effective, tender, maternal influence which she exercises so lovingly over all her children. She is Queen because she is mother. As Saint Louis de Montfort explains it, "Mary...cannot make her residence in (souls) as God the Father ordered her to do and as their mother, form, nourish and bring them forth to eternal life...unless she has a right and a domination over souls by a singular grace of the Most High...and so we can call her...the Queen of All Hearts" (*True Devotion* 37-38).

Consecration to Christ the King is the logical conclusion of meditating on this final mystery of the rosary. And we must entrust this consecration to Mary, our Mother and our Queen. Total consecration to Jesus through Mary is, as Saint Louis de Montfort explains it, nothing less than a perfect renewal of our baptism when we were first plunged into Christ Jesus, Son of Mary. The rosary calls for this practical, lived-out response on every level of our personality to infinite triune Love yearning to share life with us. We must be like Mary of the first joyful mystery: men and women freely consecrated to the Lord.

The last mystery of the rosary is, then, the jubilant celebration of the final scene of salvation history when Christ the King will come again in glory. At his right hand will be the queen-mother, Mary, welcoming all the disciples of the Lord into eternal glory. The queenship of Mary is the sure sign of our ultimate goal when we also shall reign with the Lord. Meditating on this concluding movement of the great rosary symphony, we not only adore Christ the King, we not only venerate the Queen, who by grace so uniquely shares in Her Son's royalty, but we contemplate our final destiny and that of all creation:

"Hallelujah! For the Lord our God the Almighty reigns...and his servants shall worship him, they shall see his face and his name shall be on their foreheads...and they shall reign forever and ever" (Rev 19:6; 22:3-5).

The last note of the rosary is the regal, victorious cry of the *Book of Revelation:*

"Amen! Blessing and glory and wisdom and thanksgiving and honor and power and might be to our God for ever and ever! Amen! (Rev 7:12).

May the grace of the mystery of the Coronation
of the most blessed Virgin
come down into our hearts.

APPENDIX

I

POPE PAUL VI ON THE ROSARY

Excerpts from Paul VI's
Devotion to the Blessed Virgin Mary, 42-55

42. We wish now, venerable Brothers, to dwell for a moment on the renewal of the pious practice which has been called "the compendium of the entire gospel": the rosary. To this our predecessors have devoted close attention and care. On many occasions they have recommended its frequent recitation, encouraged its diffusion, explained its nature, recognized its suitability for fostering contemplative prayer — prayer of both praise and petition — and recalled its intrinsic effectiveness for promoting christian life and apostolic commitment.

44. [In recent times] the gospel inspiration of the rosary has appeared more clearly: the rosary draws from the gospel the presentation of the mysteries and its main formulas. As it moves from the Angel's joyful greeting and the Virgin's pious assent, the rosary takes its inspiration from the gospel to suggest the attitude with which the faithful should recite it. In the harmonious succession of Hail Marys the rosary puts before us once more a fundamental mystery of the gospel — the Incarnation of the Word, contemplated at the decisive moment of the Annunciation to Mary. The rosary is thus a gospel prayer, as pastors and scholars like to define it, more today perhaps than in the past.

45. It has also been more easily seen how the orderly and gradual unfolding of the rosary reflects the very way in

which the Word of God, mercifully entering into human affairs, brought about the Redemption. The rosary considers in harmonious succession the principal salvific events accomplished in Christ, from his virginal conception and the mysteries of his childhood to the culminating moments of the Passover — the blessed Passion and the glorious Resurrection — and to the effects of this on the infant church on the day of Pentecost, and on the Virgin Mary when at the end of her earthly life she was assumed body and soul into her heavenly home. It has also been observed that the division of the mysteries of the rosary into three parts not only adheres strictly to the chronological order of the facts but above all reflects the plan of the original proclamation of the faith and sets forth once more the mystery of Christ in the very way in which it is seen by Saint Paul in the celebrated "hymn" of the Letter to the Philippians — kenosis, death and exaltation (2:6-11).

46. As a gospel prayer, centered on the mystery of the redemptive Incarnation, the rosary is, therefore, a prayer with a clearly Christological orientation. Its most characteristic element, in fact, the litany-like succession of Hail Marys, becomes in itself an unceasing praise of Christ who is the ultimate object of both the Angel's announcement and of the greeting of the Mother of John the Baptist: "Blessed is the fruit of your womb" (Lk 1:42). We would go further and say that the succession of Hail Marys constitutes the warp on which is woven the contemplation of the mysteries. The Jesus that each Hail Mary recalls is the same Jesus whom the succession of the mysteries proposes to us — now as the Son of God, now as the son of the Virgin — at his birth in a stable at Bethlehem, at his presentation by his Mother in the Temple, as a youth full of zeal for his Father's affairs, as the Redeemer in agony in the garden, scourged and crowned with thorns, carrying the

cross and dying on Calvary; risen from the dead and ascended to the glory of the Father to send forth the gift of the Spirit. As is well known, at one time there was a custom, still preserved in certain places, of adding to the name of Jesus in each Hail Mary a reference to the mystery being contemplated. And this was done precisely in order to help contemplation and to make the mind and the voice act in unison.

47. There has also been felt with greater urgency the need to point out once more the importance of a further essential element in the rosary, in addition to the value of the elements of praise and petition, namely the element of contemplation. Without this the rosary is a body without a soul, and its recitation is in danger of becoming a mechanical repetition of formulas and of going counter to the warning of Christ: "And in praying do not heap up empty phrases as the Gentiles do; for they think that they will be heard for their many words" (Mt 6:7). By its nature the recitation of the rosary calls for a quiet rhythm and a lingering pace, helping the individual to meditate on the mysteries of the Lord's life as seen through the eyes of her who was closest to the Lord. In this way the unfathomable riches of these mysteries are unfolded.

48. Finally, as a result of modern reflection the relationships between the liturgy and the rosary have been more clearly understood. On the one hand it has been emphasized that the rosary is as it were a branch sprung from the ancient trunk of the christian liturgy, the Psalter of the Blessed Virgin whereby the humble were associated in the church's hymn of praise and universal intercession. On the other hand it has been noted that this development occurred at a time — the last period of the Middle Ages — when the liturgical spirit was in decline and the faithful were turning

from the liturgy towards a devotion to Christ's humanity and to the Blessed Virgin Mary, a devotion favoring a certain external sentiment of piety. Not many years ago some people began to express the desire to see the rosary included among the rites of the liturgy while other people, anxious to avoid repetition of former pastoral mistakes, unjustifiably disregarded the rosary. Today the problem can easily be solved in the light of the principles of the Constitution (of Vatican II) *Sacrosanctum Concilium*. Liturgical celebrations and the pious practice of the rosary must neither be set in opposition to one another nor considered as being identical. The more an expression of prayer preserves its own true nature and individual characteristics the more fruitful it becomes. Once the pre-eminent value of liturgical rites has been reaffirmed it will not be difficult to appreciate the fact that the rosary is a practice of piety which easily harmonizes with the liturgy. In fact, like the liturgy, it is of a community nature, draws its inspiration from Sacred Scripture and is oriented towards the mystery of Christ. The commemoration in the liturgy and the contemplative remembrance proper to the rosary, although existing on essentially different planes of reality, have as their object the same salvific events wrought by Christ. The former presents anew, under the veil of signs and operative in a hidden way, the great mysteries of our redemption. The latter, by means of devout contemplation, recalls these same mysteries to the mind of the person praying and stimulates the will to draw from them the norms of living. Once this substantial difference has been established, it is not difficult to understand that the rosary is an exercise of piety that draws its motivating force from the liturgy and leads naturally back to it, if practiced in conformity with its original inspiration. It does not however become part of the liturgy. In fact meditation on the mysteries of the rosary, by familiarizing the hearts and minds of the faithful with the mysteries of Christ, can be an excellent preparation for the celebration of these same mysteries in the liturgical action and can also become a continuing echo thereof. However, it is a mistake to recite the rosary during the celebration of the liturgy, though unfortunately this practice still persists here and there.

49. The rosary of the Blessed Virgin Mary, according to the tradition accepted by our predecessor Saint Pius V and authoritatively taught by him, consists of various elements disposed in an organic fashion:

2) Contemplation, in communion with Mary, of a series of *mysteries of salvation*, wisely distributed into three cycles. The mysteries express the joy of the messianic times, the salvific suffering of Christ and the glory of the Risen Lord which fills the church. This contemplation by its very nature encourages practical reflection and provides stimulating norms for living.

b) The Lord's Prayer, or Our Father, which by reason of its immense value is at the basis of christian prayer and ennobles that prayer in its various expressions.

c) The litany-like succession of the Hail Mary, which is made up of the Angel's greeting to the Virgin (cf Lk 1:28) and of Elizabeth's greeting (cf. Lk 1:42), followed by the ecclesial supplication, Holy Mary. The continued series of Hail Marys is the special characteristic of the rosary, and their number in the full and typical number of one hundred and fifty, presents a certain analogy with the Psalter and is an element that goes back to the very origin of this exercise of piety. But this number, divided, according to a well-tried custom, into decades attached to the individual mysteries, is distributed in the three cycles already mentioned, thus giving rise to the rosary of fifty Hail Marys as we know it. This latter has entered into use as the normal measure of the pious practice and as such has been adopted by popular piety and approval by papal authority which also enriched it with numerous indulgences.

d) The doxology Glory be to the Father which, in conformity with an orientation common to christian piety concludes the prayer with the glorifying of God who is one and three, from whom, through whom and in whom all things have their being (cf. Rom 11:36).

50. These are the elements of the rosary. Each has its own particular character which, wisely understood and appreciated, should be reflected in the recitation, in order that the rosary may express all its richness and variety. Thus the recitation will be grave and suppliant during the Lord's Prayer, lyrical and full of praise during the tranquil succession of Hail Marys, contemplative in the recollected meditation on the mysteries and full of adoration during the doxology. This applies to all the ways in which the rosary is usually recited: privately, in intimate recollection with the Lord; in community, in the family or in groups of the faithful gathered together to ensure the special presence of the Lord (cf. Mt 18:20); or publicly, in assemblies in which the ecclesial community is invited.

51. In recent times certain exercises of piety have been created which take their inspiration from the rosary. Among such exercises we wish to draw attention to and recommend those which insert into the ordinary celebration of the Word of God some elements of the rosary, such as meditation on the mysteries and litany-like repetition of the angel's greeting to Mary. In this way these elements gain in importance, since they are found in the context of Bible readings, illustrated with a homily, accompanied by silent pauses and emphasized with song. We are happy to know that such practices have helped to promote a more complete understanding of the spiritual riches of the rosary

itself and have served to restore esteem for its recitation among youth associations and movements.

52. We now desire as a continuation of the thought of our predecessors, to recommend strongly the recitation of the family rosary. The Second Vatican Council has pointed out how the family, the primary and vital cell of society, "shows itself to be the domestic sanctuary of the church through the mutual affection of its members and the common prayer they offer to God." The christian family is thus seen to be a domestic church if its members, each according to his proper place and tasks, all together promote justice, practice works of mercy, devote themselves to helping their brethren, take part in the apostolate of the wider local community and play their part in its liturgical worship. This will be all the more true if together they offer up prayers to God. If this element of common prayer were missing, the family would lack its very character as a domestic church. Thus there must logically follow a concrete effort to reinstate communal prayer in family life if there is to be a restoration of the theological concept of the family as the domestic church.

53. In accordance with the directives of the Council, the *Institutio Generalis de Liturgia Horarum* rightly numbers the family among the groups in which the Divine Office can suitably be celebrated in community: "It is fitting...that the family, as a domestic sanctuary of the church, should not only offer prayers to God in common, but also, according to circumstances, should recite parts of the Liturgy of the Hours, in order to be more intimately linked with the church." No avenue should be left unexplored to ensure that this clear and practical recommendation finds within christian families growing and joyful acceptance.

54. But there is no doubt, that after the celebration of the Liturgy of the Hours, the high point which family prayer can reach, the rosary should be considered as one of the best and most efficacious prayers in common that the christian family is invited to recite. We like to think and sincerely hope, that when the family gathering becomes a time of prayer the rosary is a frequent and favored manner of praying. We are well aware that the changed conditions of life today do not make family gatherings easy and that even when such a gathering is possible many circumstances make it difficult to turn it into an occasion of prayer. There is no doubt of the difficulty. But it is characteristic of the christian in his manner of life not to give in to circumstances but to overcome them, not to succumb but to make an effort. Families which want to live in full measure the vocation and spirituality proper to the christian family must therefore devote all their energies to overcoming the pressures that hinder family gatherings and prayer in common.

55. In concluding these observations, which give proof of the concern and esteem which the Apostolic See has for the rosary of the Blessed Virgin Mary, we desire at the same time to recommend that this very worthy devotion should not be propagated in a way that is too one-sided or exclusive. The rosary is an excellent prayer but the faithful should feel serenely free in its regard. They should be drawn to its calm recitation by its intrinsic appeal.

Taken from *L'Osservatore Romano*, English Weekly Edition, 4-4-74.

Official Vatican Translation

II

POPULAR METHOD OF RECITING THE ROSARY ACCORDING TO SAINT LOUIS DE MONTFORT

I unite with all the saints in heaven, with all the just on earth and with all the faithful here present. I unite with you, O my Jesus in order to praise worthily your holy Mother and to praise you in her and through her. I renounce all the distractions which I may have during this rosary which I wish to say with modesty, attention and devotion as if it were to be the last of my life.

We offer you, O most Holy Trinity, this *Creed* in honor of all the mysteries of our Faith; this *Our Father* and these three *Hail Marys* in honor of the unity of your Essence and the Trinity of your Persons. We ask of you a lively faith, a firm hope and an ardent charity. Amen.

I believe in God, etc.

THE FIVE JOYFUL MYSTERIES

1. *The Annunciation*

We offer you, O Lord Jesus, this first decade in honor of your Incarnation in Mary's womb, and we ask of you, through this mystery and through her intercession, a profound humility. Amen.

Our Father, etc., ten *Hail Mary's.*

May the grace of the mystery of the Annunciation come down into our souls. Amen.

2. *The Visitation*

We offer you, O Lord Jesus, this second decade in honor of

107

the Visitation of your holy Mother to her cousin St. Elizabeth and the sanctification of St. John the Baptist, and we ask of you, through this mystery and through the intercession of your holy Mother, charity towards our neighbor. Amen.

Our Father, etc., ten *Hail Mary's.*

May the grace of the mystery of the Visitation come down into our souls. Amen.

3. *The Nativity*

We offer you, O Lord Jesus, this third decade in honor of your Nativity in the stable of Bethlehem, and we ask of you, through this mystery and through the intercession of your holy Mother, detachment from the things of the world, contempt of riches and love of poverty. Amen.

Our Father, etc., ten *Hail Mary's.*

May the grace of the Mystery of the Nativity come down into our souls. Amen.

4. *The Presentation in the Temple*

We offer you, O Lord Jesus, this fourth decade in honor of your Presentation in the Temple and the Purification of Mary, and we ask of you, through this mystery and through the intercession of your holy Mother, purity of body and soul. Amen.

Our Father, etc., ten *Hail Mary's.*

May the grace of the mystery of the Presentation in the Temple come down into our souls. Amen.

5. *The Finding of Our Lord in the Temple*

We offer you, O Lord Jesus, this fifth decade in honor of Mary's finding you in the temple, and we ask of you, through this mystery and through her intercession, the gift of true wisdom. Amen.

Our Father, etc., ten *Hail Mary's.*

May the grace of the mystery of the Finding of Our Lord in the Temple come down into our souls. Amen.

THE FIVE SORROWFUL MYSTERIES

1. *The Agony in the Garden*

We offer you, O Lord Jesus, this sixth decade in honor of your Agony in the Garden of Olives, and we ask of you, through this mystery and through the intercession of your holy Mother, contrition for our sins. Amen.

Our Father, etc., ten *Hail Mary's.*

May the grace of the mystery of the Agony in the Garden come down into our souls. Amen.

2. *The Scourging*

We offer you, O Lord Jesus, this seventh decade in honor of your cruel Scourging, and we ask of you, through this mystery and through the intercession of your holy Mother, the grace of mortifying our senses. Amen.

Our Father, etc., ten *Hail Mary's.*

May the grace of the mystery of the Scourging come down into our souls. Amen.

3. *The Crowning with Thorns*

We offer you, O Lord Jesus, this eighth decade in honor of your being crowned with thorns and we ask of you, through this mystery and through the intercession of your holy Mother contempt of the world. Amen.

Our Father, etc., ten *Hail Mary's.*

May the grace of the mystery of the Crowning with Thorns come down into our souls. Amen.

4. *The Carrying of the Cross*

We offer you, O Lord Jesus, this ninth decade in honor of your carrying of the cross and we ask of you, through this mystery and through the intercession of your holy Mother, patience in bearing our crosses. Amen.

Our Father, etc., ten *Hail Mary's.*

May the grace of the mystery of the Carrying of the Cross come down into our souls. Amen.

5. *The Crucifixion*

We offer you, O Lord Jesus, this tenth decade in honor of your Crucifixion and ignominious death on Calvary; we ask of you, through this mystery and through the intercession of your holy Mother, the conversion of sinners, the perseverance of the just and the relief of the souls in purgatory. Amen.

Our Father, etc., ten *Hail Mary's.*

May the grace of the mystery of the Crucifixion come down into our souls. Amen.

THE FIVE GLORIOUS MYSTERIES

1. *The Resurrection*

We offer you, O Lord Jesus, this eleventh decade in honor of your glorious Resurrection, and we ask of you, through this mystery and through the intercession of your holy Mother, love of God and fervor in your service. Amen.

Our Father, etc., ten *Hail Mary's.*

May the grace of the mystery of the Resurrection come down into our souls. Amen.

2. *The Ascension*

We offer you, O Lord Jesus, this twelfth decade in honor of your triumphant Ascension and we ask of you, through this mystery and through the intercession of your holy Mother, an ardent desire for heaven, our true home. Amen.

Our Father, etc., ten *Hail Mary's.*

May the grace of the mystery of the Ascension come down into our souls. Amen.

3. *The Descent of the Holy Spirit*

We offer you, O Lord Jesus, this thirteenth decade in honor of the mystery of Pentecost, and we ask of you, through this mystery and through the intercession of your holy Mother, the coming of the Holy Spirit into our souls. Amen.

Our Father, etc., ten *Hail Mary's.*

May the grace of the mystery of Pentecost come down into our souls. Amen.

4. *The Assumption*

We offer you, O Lord Jesus, this fourteenth decade in honor of the resurrection and triumphant Assumption of your holy Mother into heaven and we ask of you, through this mystery and through her intercession, a tender devotion for so good a Mother. Amen.

Our Father, etc., ten *Hail Mary's.*

May the grace of the mystery of the Assumption come down into our souls. Amen.

5. *The Coronation of the Blessed Virgin*

We offer you, O Lord Jesus, this fifteenth decade in honor of the Coronation of your holy Mother, and we ask you, through this mystery and through her intercession, perseverance in grace and a crown of glory hereafter. Amen.

Our Father, etc., ten *Hail Mary's*.

May the grace of the mystery of the Coronation of the Blessed Virgin come down into our souls. Amen.

CLOSING PRAYER

Hail Mary, beloved Daughter of the Eternal Father, admirable Mother of the Son, faithful Spouse of the Holy Spirit, august Temple of the most Holy Trinity! Hail, sovereign princess, to whom all owe subjection in heaven and on earth! Hail, sure refuge of sinners, our Lady of mercy, who has never refused any request. All sinful though I am, I cast myself at your feet and beseech you to obtain from Jesus, your beloved Son, contrition and pardon for all my sins, as well as the gift of Divine Wisdom. I consecrate myself entirely to you with all that I have. I choose you today for my Mother and Mistress. Treat me, then, as the least of your children and the most obedient of your servants. Listen, my princess, listen to the sighs of a heart that desires to love and serve you faithfully. Let it never be said that of all those who have had recourse to you, I was the first to be abandoned. O my hope, O my life, O my faithful and immaculate Virgin Mary, defend me, nourish me, hear me, teach me and save me. Amen.

Praised, Adored and Loved Be Jesus in the Most Holy Sacrament of the Altar, Forever and Ever!

(See *God Alone, The Collected Works of St. Louis Marie de Montfort*, pp. 233-259, for the various methods recommended by St. Louis de Montfort)